guilford courthouse 1781

lord cornwallis's ruinous victory

ANGUS KONSTAM

guilford courthouse 1781

lord cornwallis's ruinous victory

Praeger Illustrated Military History Series

PRAEGER

Westport, Connecticut
London

Library of Congress Cataloging-in-Publication Data

Konstam, Angus.
    Guilford Courthouse, 1781: Lord Cornwallis's ruinous victory / Angus Konstam.
       p. cm. – (Praeger illustrated military history, ISSN 1547-206X)
    Originally published: Oxford: Osprey, 2002.
    Includes bibliographical references and index.
    ISBN 0-275-98461-3 (alk. paper)
    1. Guilford Courthouse, Battle of, N.C., 1781. 2. Guilford Courthouse, Battle of,
    N.C., 1781 – Pictorial works. I. Title. II. Series.
    E241.G9K66   2004
    973.3'37–dc22   2004050386

British Library Cataloguing in Publication Data is available.

First published in paperback in 2002 by Osprey Publishing Limited, Elms Court,
Chapel Way, Botley, Oxford OX2 9LP. All rights reserved.

Copyright © 2004 by Osprey Publishing Limited

Library of Congress Catalog Card Number: 2004050386
ISBN: 0-275-98461-3
ISSN: 1547-206X

Praeger Publishers, 88 Post Road West, Westport, CT 06881
An imprint of Greenwood Publishing Group, Inc.
www.praeger.com

Printed in China through World Print Ltd.

The paper used in this book complies with the Permanent Paper Standard issued
by the National Information Standards Organization (Z39.48-1984).

10   9   8   7   6   5   4   3   2   1

ILLUSTRATED BY: Adam Hook

CONTENTS

KEY TO MILITARY SYMBOLS

INTRODUCTION

In the years before the bloody clash between Generals Greene and Cornwallis at Guilford Courthouse, this tranquil rural hamlet in North Carolina's piedmont was just an obscure road junction in a remote part of an under-developed colony. The name derived from the building on the forest road that served as the seat of justice for the county, the court sitting in quarterly sessions. The events of that cold spring morning of 15 March 1781, however, ensured that the name of Guilford Courthouse became synonymous with a bloody battle, an American defeat and ultimately, with a major milestone on the path that led to final American victory in the war for independence.

For months, the British army of 2,000 regular troops commanded by Lieutenant-General Earl Cornwallis had tried to force an American army led by Major-General Nathaniel Greene to meet them in battle. The British had hoped that a decisive victory would secure British control over the two colonies of the Carolinas, and allow Cornwallis to carry the war north, into the Commonwealth of Virginia, the colony which he regarded as the keystone of the Americas. By early March, militia from Virginia had reinforced Nathaniel Greene's army, and the American commander decided to give the British the battle they sought so desperately. For both sides, the stakes were high, and the troops understood the importance of their actions. On the night of 14 March 1781, Greene's men camped around Guilford Courthouse, and the following morning, as the British marched the 12 miles from their

RIGHT **Although very few cavalrymen were used during the American War of Independence, both General Cornwallis and General Greene made full use of their light dragoons to harry the enemy, and to attack his outposts during the campaign for the Carolinas.**

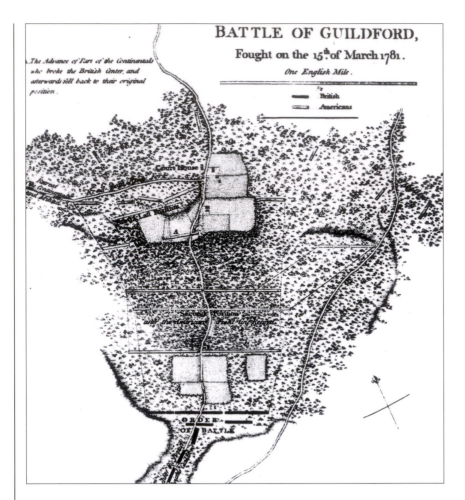

BATTLE OF GUILDFORD,
Fought on the 15th of March 1781.

One English Mile.

British
Americans

The Advance of Part of the Continentals who broke the British Center, and afterwards fell back to their original position.

ORDER OF BATTLE

The battle of Guilford Courthouse, 1781, was fought over woods and small clearings, and no military engineer could replicate the confused nature of the fighting. This map was first produced to accompany Banastre Tarleton's memoirs of the southern campaign.

bivouac at Deep Friends Meeting House, the General arrayed his troops to block their path. Cornwallis raced his men forward through the cold pre-dawn darkness until his troops met the enemy in battle. The result was one of the most close-fought and bitterly contested engagements of

Cornwallis rejected the use of a conventional artillery train during the campaign, due to the appalling transportation problems the guns would have encountered in the Carolina backcountry. Instead, he relied on light "galloper guns" for support.

One of the most dramatic incidents during the campaign was the charge against the British Foot Guards by Colonel Washington's Continental Dragoons. The charge almost decided the outcome of the battle, but the resolve of both Cornwallis and his guardsmen saved the day.

the American War of Independence. Although the engagement was a British victory, it was an extremely costly one. Cornwallis lost over a quarter of his small army in those few hours on 15 March 1781. Worse still, although Greene's American army was defeated, its core of hardened Continental Army regulars remained intact, ready to fight another day.

In the aftermath of this pyrrhic victory, Cornwallis was forced to abandon his plans to carry the war into Virginia, and his battered little army had to retire to a friendly haven to recover. This British move to Wilmington, North Carolina, immediately after the battle allowed Cornwallis to re-establish his lines of supply and communication, but it also left the rest of North Carolina and South Carolina exposed to enemy attack. Ultimately, the achievements of Charleston and Camden were reversed, as Greene led his army back south, attacking British and Loyalist outposts in South Carolina, and the area of British control was reduced to the coastal enclaves around Charleston and Georgetown. The second strategic effect of the battle of Guilford Courthouse would have more dramatic consequences. While his army lay encamped around Wilmington, Cornwallis reconsidered his plans for an invasion of Virginia, hoping to draw Greene's army into another battle, and to deny the Americans the benefit of succour from the fertile and prosperous colony. Instead, Cornwallis and his army found themselves outnumbered and trapped at Yorktown, on Virginia's York River. Most of the British troops who surrendered with Cornwallis on 17 October 1781 were veterans of the battle of Guilford Courthouse. For them as well as for their commander, that battle, fought in the wilds of North Carolina just over seven months before, marked a turning point in the war. It was the first step on the road to a dramatic American victory, and to the independence of the United States of America.

CHRONOLOGY

THE COURSE OF THE WAR, 1775–80

1775
19 April Skirmishes at Lexington and Concord

20 April Commencement of the Siege of Boston

17 June Battle of Bunker Hill. British victory

1776
26 February Battle of Moore's Creek Bridge, SC. American victory

17 March British evacuation from Boston

1 June–21 July British attack on Fort Sullivan, SC repulsed

4 July Signature of the Declaration of Independence

August Campaign for New York

27 August Battle of Long Island

16 September Battle of Harlem Heights

17 September British capture New York

28 October Battle of White Plains

November–December American retreat through New Jersey

25 December Skirmish at Trenton. American victory

1777
2 January Skirmish at Princeton. American victory

13 June General Burgoyne begins his advance on the Hudson Valley

11 September Battle of Brandywine. British victory

19 September Battle of Freeman's Farm (1st Saratoga). American victory

26 September British capture Philadelphia

4 October Battle of Germantown. British victory

7 October Battle of Bemis Heights (2nd Saratoga). American victory

9 October Burgoyne's British army surrendered at Saratoga

1778
18 June British abandon Philadelphia

28 June Battle of Monmouth. No clear victor

29 December British land near Savannah, GA, and capture city

1779
19 June Skirmish at Stono Ferry, North Carolina. American victory

3 September–28 October Siege of Savannah. British victory.

THE WAR IN THE CAROLINAS
26 December General Clinton sails from New York, bound for Charleston, SC

1780
11 February British land at Edisto Island, south of Charleston

14 April Skirmish at Monck's Corner, SC. British victory

11 February–12 May Siege of Charleston

12 May General Lincoln surrenders Charleston to the British

29 May Skirmish at Waxhaws, SC. British victory

20 June Skirmish at Ramseur's Mill, SC. American victory

Skirmish at Williamson's Plantation, SC. American victory

1 July Georgetown, South Carolina captured by the British

1 August Attack on Loyalist outpost at Rocky Mount, SC repulsed

5 August Attack on Loyalist outpost at Hanging Rock, SC repulsed

16 August Battle of Camden. British victory

25 September British capture Charlotte, NC

7 October Battle of King's Mountain. American victory, Major Patrick Ferguson killed

1781

17 January Battle of Cowpens. American victory

THE GUILFORD COURTHOUSE CAMPAIGN, JANUARY–MARCH, 1781

18 January Cornwallis' army reinforced by Maj-Gen Leslie's command

19 January British army starts off in pursuit of Morgan

23 January Morgan crosses the Catawba River

24 January Cornwallis reaches Ramseur's Mill

30 January Greene and Morgan join forces

1 February Cornwallis storms Cowan's Ford

2 February Greene enters Salisbury

3 February Both armies separated by the Yadkin River

4 February The Americans retreat from the Yadkin to Guilford Courthouse

9 February British enter Salem

10 February Americans march north from Guilford Courthouse

13 February Skirmish between Tarleton and Lee's cavalry

15 February The last American troops cross the Dan River

16 February Cornwallis marches to Hillsborough

18 February American light troops recross the Dan River

22 February Greene leads main army back across the Dan River

25 February Pyle's Massacre

26 February Cornwallis moves his camp to Stinking Quarter Creek

6 March Skirmish at Weitzel's Mill

10 March Greene's army reinforced by militia

14 March Greene marches his army south towards Guilford Courthouse

Cornwallis prepares to march to confront Greene at Guilford Courthouse

Skirmish between Tarleton and Lee's cavalry on the New Garden Road

THE BATTLE OF GUILFORD COURTHOUSE, 15 MARCH 1781

(Note: All times given are approximate, based on often contradictory evidence).

2.00am American patrols note activity in the British camp

3.00am Cornwallis's army begins its march up the New Garden Road

4.00am First clash between the British advanced guard and American patrols

4.40am Skirmish to the east of the New Garden Meeting House

5.00am Greene's army breakfasts, then moves into their allotted positions

10.00am Lee's advanced guard rejoins the main American army

Noon The British advanced guard sights the first American line

12.10pm American artillery opens fire

12.40pm The artillery duel ceases as the British deploy

1.00pm The British advance towards the first American line

1.15pm The North Carolina militia rout

1.40pm The Second Line is attacked

2.15pm The Virginia militia rout

2.30pm Lee's Legion make a stand to the south of the battlefield

2.45pm The British launch their assault on the Third Line

3.00pm Col Washington and LtCol Howard counterattack

3.15pm Cornwallis fires his artillery into the melee

3.30pm Greene gives the order to retire from the field

The last shots are fired in the southern portion of the battlefield

THE AFTERMATH OF GUILFORD COURTHOUSE, MARCH 1781–DECEMBER 1783

16 March Greene's army at the Speedwell Ironworks. The British bury their dead

18 March Cornwallis begins march to the east

20 March Greene's army re-occupies the battlefield

27 March Greene and Cornwallis almost clash at Ramsey's Mill

29 March Greene turns his army south into South Carolina

7 April Cornwallis's army enters Wilmington

25 April Battle of Hobkirk's Hill, SC. British victory

12 May Cornwallis's army enters Virginia

20 May Cornwallis joins forces with Benedict Arnold in Petersburg, VA

21 August Washington and Rochambeau march south from New York State

5 September Naval Battle of the Chesapeake

8 September Battle of Eutaw Springs, SC British victory

14 September Washington reaches Williamsburg, VA

28 September Start of the siege of Yorktown, VA

19 October Cornwallis's British army surrenders at Yorktown

1782

11 July British abandon Savannah, GA

30 November First peace treaty signed in Paris

14 December British abandon Charleston, SC

1783

19 April Congress proclaims an end to hostilities with Britain

3 September Final peace treaty signed

25 November British abandon New York

23 December General Washington steps down as Commander-in-Chief

BACKGROUND TO THE CAMPAIGN

Sir Henry Clinton (1739–1812) was the British Commander-in-Chief in the Americas, responsible directly to the king and his ministers for the prosecution of the war. It was Clinton's plan to move the theatre of war to the southern colonies after the stalemate of 1777.

The events that led to the Guilford Courthouse campaign were set in train in late 1777, when the British government decided to change the course of the war in the American colonies. Since the outbreak of the American Revolution in 1775, the conflict had largely been limited to the northern colonies. Despite British initiatives, the war had reached a stalemate, so in the summer of 1777 a two-pronged attack was planned against both Philadelphia and the Hudson River. The northern offensive led to the surrender of a British army commanded by General John Burgoyne at Saratoga, New York. To make matters worse, although the southern offensive captured Philadelphia, General Washington's Continental Army remained intact, and was given time to regroup and to rebuild its forces. To add to the misery of the British government, the French had allied themselves with the American rebels, and declared war on Britain. It was clear to the government that the entry of France into the war would alter the strategic balance. As the Commander-in-Chief of the British Army in the Americas, Sir Henry Clinton decided that drastic measures were needed to regain the initiative and bring the war to a speedy conclusion, before the full weight of the French could influence the conflict. The war in the northern colonies had reached a stalemate, so Clinton decided to focus on the southern colonies, from Florida (safely in British hands) to Virginia. By launching an attack in the south, Clinton could take advantage of the strategic maneuverability of his army, as it could be transported by sea far faster than Washington could march an army down the eastern seaboard of the colonies. This meant the British would achieve a local superiority in numbers, and could seize the region before Congress could send an army south. Politicians and ministers in London approved the notion in principle, and it was left to Sir Henry to devise the best way in which his strategy could be put into effect. Until this point, the south had been a virtual backwater in the war. This was about to change, and the Carolinas would be plunged into a bitterly fought civil war.

The campaign would mark the first British initiative in the south since 1776, when a loyalist force of former Highlanders was defeated at Moore's Creek Bridge north of Wilmington, North Carolina. Incidentally, the battle saw the only Highland charge ever attempted in the Americas, and the result was a disaster for the Loyalists. In February of the same year the British made a half-hearted and ultimately abortive attack against Fort Sullivan guarding the sea approaches to Charleston, South Carolina. The failure of both the local loyalists and the British to make any impression led the British commanders to look elsewhere for their victories. Clinton's decision led to a reappraisal of the possibilities offered by the southern colonies to the forces of the crown.

The decision to launch an attack against the southern colonies in 1778 was based on two largely flawed premises. The first was that given

13

ABOVE **General George Washington (1732–1799), the Commander-in-Chief of the Continental Army, was asked by Congress to suggest a replacement for Major-General Gates as commander of the southern theatre. His decision to send Major-General Greene was an inspired decision that helped alter the course of the war.**

ABOVE, RIGHT **The sentiment "Unite or Die" is represented here by this popular cartoon. Congress recognized the seriousness of the situation in the southern states following the loss of Charleston, but the northern states were slow to place resources and supplies at the disposal of their southern compatriots.**

British naval supremacy, an overwhelming force could be brought to bear against a particular target, and the poor land communications in the south meant that American reinforcements would be hard-pressed to influence the outcome of a campaign. The problem with this was that the entry of France into the war also brought the French fleet into the arena, and, in 1780–81 at least, it was large and experienced enough to wrest control of the seas from the British in the coastal waters of the southern colonies. Second, the British assumed from the information supplied by former British governors to the region and from prominent local loyalists that a significant portion of the local population were loyal to the Crown. The real situation was very different. Although up to a third of the population in Georgia and the Carolinas may have had loyalist sympathies, a string of defeats had left these men reluctant to renew the struggle against their friends and neighbours.

The first British objective was the city of Savannah, Georgia, which was captured after a short engagement on 29 December 1778. It was soon followed by the fall of Sunbury and Augusta, and the Royal Governor was returned to rule the colony during early 1779. The British press boasted of having taken "the first strip and star out of the rebel flag," and the colony provided a base for raids into the Carolinas. Major-General Benjamin Lincoln foiled a British attempt to seize Charleston at the skirmish at Stono Ferry (19 June 1779), and after calling on the French for assistance, the American commander duly marched south to besiege Savannah. In early September he was joined by a detachment of 3,500 French troops, and the allies lay siege to the city. All attempts to capture Savannah were foiled, and the attacks were repulsed with heavy losses. In disgust, the French abandoned the siege in October.

This operation was a foretaste of greater things to come. General Clinton decided to launch an attack on Charleston, South Carolina. His forces landed on Edisto Island to the south of the city on 11 February 1780, and despite the presence of Major-General Lincoln and his army of 5,500 men, the Americans were unable to prevent the investment of the city. By the start of April, Lincoln's men were bottled up in a besieged city, and just five weeks later, on 12 May, Charleston surrendered. This was the greatest American capitulation of the war, and at a stroke it stripped the Carolinas of the means of their own defence.

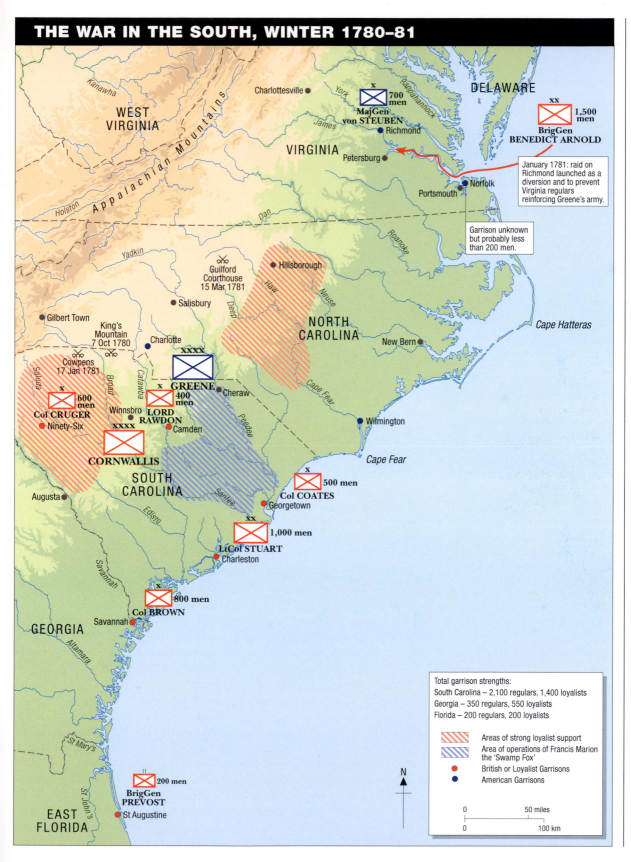

THE WAR IN THE SOUTH, WINTER 1780–81

WEST VIRGINIA

Charlottesville

DELAWARE

x 700 men
MajGen von STEUBEN

xx 1,500 men
BrigGen BENEDICT ARNOLD

VIRGINIA

Richmond

Petersburg

Portsmouth Norfolk

January 1781: raid on Richmond launched as a diversion and to prevent Virginia regulars reinforcing Greene's army.

Garrison unknown but probably less than 200 men.

Kanawha

Holston

Appalachian Mountains

Yadkin

Dan

Roanoke

Hillsborough

Guilford Courthouse 15 Mar 1781

Salisbury

Gilbert Town

King's Mountain 7 Oct 1780

Charlotte

Haw

Neuse

NORTH CAROLINA

Cape Hatteras

New Bern

Cowpens 17 Jan 1781

xxxx GREENE 400 men

Cheraw

Cape Fear

x 600 men
Col CRUGER
Ninety-Six

Winnsbro

x LORD RAWDON
Camden

Wilmington

xxxx CORNWALLIS

SOUTH CAROLINA

Peedee

Cape Fear

Saluda

Broad

Catawba

Augusta

Edisto

Santee

x 500 men
Col COATES
Georgetown

xx 1,000 men
LtCol STUART
Charleston

Savannah

x 800 men
Col BROWN
Savannah

GEORGIA

Altamara

Total garrison strengths:
South Carolina – 2,100 regulars, 1,400 loyalists
Georgia – 350 regulars, 550 loyalists
Florida – 200 regulars, 200 loyalists

Areas of strong loyalist support
Area of operations of Francis Marion the 'Swamp Fox'
British or Loyalist Garrisons
American Garrisons

St Mary's

St John's

ll 200 men
BrigGen PREVOST
St Augustine

EAST FLORIDA

N

0   50 miles
0   100 km

15

An American Farmstead during the American Revolutionary period. Many of the officers in both the Continental army and the southern militias were farmers with small but prosperous holdings such as this one. (Abby Aldrich Rockefeller Folk Art Center, Williamsburg, VA)

Lieutenant-General Charles, Earl Cornwallis (1738–1805) was a gifted professional soldier, and probably the only British field commander with the skill needed to ensure victory in the southern campaign.

The fall of Charleston and the humiliation of an American patriot army did much to encourage loyalist sympathizers in South Carolina, and as Cornwallis sent out columns of troops from Charleston into the hinterland, other towns fell to the British, and local loyalists flocked to join the colors. At first Clinton followed a political policy of appeasement, offering to pardon former patriots if they swore not to rebel again. For some reason this policy changed on 3 June, when he issued a proclamation that, simply put, declared that the local population would be considered hostile unless they could demonstrate their loyalty to the Crown. He then departed for New York, leaving his subordinate, Cornwallis, to deal with the ramifications of this statement. Previously former patriots might have been content to remain neutral but now such a course was denied them. The effect was to drive the former rebels back into the American camp, and South Carolina was plunged into a bitter civil war, where neighbours and kin were divided on political lines. Cornwallis had been charged with safeguarding the security of South Carolina, and he set about establishing a chain of strongholds in a crescent around Charleston, at Ninety-Six, Camden and Georgetown, as well as a string of smaller outposts between them. Even these measures proved insufficient to ensure the peace and stability of the colony. To help defend these posts, Cornwallis relied on a mobile force of dragoons and light infantry commanded by Lieutenant-Colonel Banastre Tarleton, an energetic young officer with a talent for ruthless pursuit. On 29 May Tarleton struck an isolated detachment of Virginian Continental Line at Waxhaws, north of Camden. In the ensuing rout, he gained the probably undeserved reputation of having massacred his opponents after they had surrendered. From that point on the patriots referred to him as "Bloody Tarleton", and coined the phrase "Tarleton's Quarter" to justify the slaughter of loyalist prisoners. In the increasingly bloody civil war in the Carolinas, the gentlemanly rules of 18th-century warfare were swept aside in a wave of

ABOVE **Major-General Benjamin Lincoln (1733–1810) was outmanoeuvred by Sir Henry Clinton, and as a result, he was forced to surrender his entire army of 5,500 men at Charleston in May 1780, but despite this debacle he returned to serve in Washington's Continental Army the following year.**

LEFT **The flag of South Carolina flying over Fort Moultrie, the principal fort guarding Charleston Harbor. Although the British failed to capture the fort in 1776, it fell during the Siege of Charleston four years later. This engraving depicts Sergeant Jasper, a hero of the fort's defence of 1776.**

recriminations and reprisals. On 20 June Loyalist forces mustering outside the defensive perimeter were attacked and routed by local patriots at Ramseur's Mill and Williamson's Plantation, prompting support for the British cause to wane in areas that the army was unable to protect. This was followed by attacks on some of Cornwallis's chain of outposts, at Rocky Mount (1 August) and Hanging Rock four days later. Although these American assaults were repulsed, a more serious threat to the British was developing to the north. Major-General Horatio Gates, the victor of Saratoga, had been sent south at the head of a small regular army to restore American control in South Carolina. Gates had over 4,000 men under his command, including two brigades of Continental Line (1,500 men), supported by artillery and a small cavalry arm. The regulars were commanded by the experienced Bavarian soldier "Baron" de Kalb. On 27 July the Americans left their camp in North Carolina and marched on

Camden, the closest British outpost, which was commanded by Lord Rawdon. Just north of Camden, Gates bowed to pressure from his militia commanders and detached 400 men for an attack on a British supply train. This left him barely sufficient men to take on 2,200 British and Loyalist troops who marched from Camden to meet him. The two armies met during the night of 15 August, and the following morning, Cornwallis sent his men into the attack. The Virginia militia simply ran away, leaving their companions from North Carolina with an exposed flank. When they fled the field in their turn, it was left to De Kalb's regulars to save the day. After a vicious struggle they were swept aside, and their commander was mortally wounded. As for Gates, he retired as soon as the British attacked, and kept riding until he reached Charlotte, North Carolina. The second American army in the Carolinas had been crushed, leaving Cornwallis the opportunity to consider his next move.

British officers on horseback conferring during the campaign. Cornwallis was able to draw on a collection of extremely gifted brigade commanders to assist him, including Colonel Webster of the 33rd Foot, and Colonel O'Hara of the Foot Guards.

For some time the Earl Cornwallis had been convinced that the best way to defend South Carolina was to enter North Carolina and destroy the American partisan forces and remnants of Gates' army who used the colony as a base. North Carolina served as a secure base from which partisans could attack British outposts, and by clearing the region a far as the Virginia state line, Cornwallis would be able to draw on the loyalist supporters who were scattered throughout the region. Since the debacle

A British grenadier shown despatching a fallen American officer. This was the fate of the gifted "Baron" de Kalb during the final stages of the battle of Camden (1780), and his loss was a serious blow to the American cause.

at Moore's Creek Bridge over four years before they had remained mute, waiting for the opportunity to rise up and fight their neighbours. It was largely an illusion, but the notion dominated thinking in both London and in Cornwallis's camp.

Camden marked the end of a phase in the war, and the British victory ensured the security of the southern part of South Carolina. While Cornwallis planned his invasion of North Carolina in September, he still had the problem of dealing with partisans such as Francis Marion, based on the lower Peedee River, and Thomas Sumter, based between the upper reaches of the Broad and Catawba Rivers. To secure his left flank,

RIGHT **A camp of American partisans, such as the group operated by Francis Marion, based on Snow Island, on the lower reaches of South Carolina's Peedee River. Such units provided a constant source of irritation for Cornwallis as he tried to maintain his lines of communication with Charleston.**

LEFT **In the battle of Camden (1780), Lieutenant-General Cornwallis utterly routed the force of American line and militia commanded by Major-General Gates which marched south to attack him. Cornwallis's victory paved the way for the completion of his conquest of South Carolina.**

ABOVE **Francis Marion (c.1732–95). Known as the "Swamp Fox", this partisan leader operated on Cornwallis's right flank, raiding British and Loyalist outposts and supply convoys from Georgetown to Camden. His actions forced the British to deploy precious men and resources to counter his attacks.**

ABOVE, RIGHT **The battle of Moore's Creek Bridge (1776) resulted in a crushing defeat for the loyalists of North Carolina, who remained inactive until the arrival of Cornwallis. This view from the patriot lines shows the line of advance of the Highland loyalists from the creek in the far distance.**

"The British are coming!" In this print by Felix Darnley local militiamen are depicted responding to the call to arms. All the southern colonies boasted efficient well-organised militia organisations.

he detached a column of loyalist militia under the command of Major Patrick Ferguson, a gifted and energetic Scotsman who was the inventor of the Ferguson Rifle, a breech-loading masterpiece that was deemed too complicated for adoption by the army. Ferguson was charged with securing the northern portion of South Carolina, and safeguarding the region from attacks by patriot "mountainmen" descending from North Carolina's Blue Ridge Mountains. Meanwhile, Tarleton and others tried to guard Cornwallis's lines of communication with Charleston, which were threatened by Marion's men. Cornwallis began his invasion by marching from his camp in Winnsboro towards Charlotte, North Carolina, but fever among his troops delayed the advance, and the town was only captured on 26 September after a brief skirmish. By this stage Ferguson and his 1,100-strong force had moved to Gilbert Town in North Carolina, in the headwaters of the Broad River. From there he

issued an ultimatum to the "over-the-mountain men" to "desist from their opposition to British arms." If provoked, he would "lay their country waste with fire and sword." If anyone was provoked, it was the mountain men, and over 1,000 of them gathered at Quaker Meadows on the upper Catawba River, determined to end this threat to their homes. When Ferguson learned that his prey had turned on him he retreated to the southeast to link with Cornwallis's army. When it became clear his pursuers were gaining, he stopped at King's Mountain in South Carolina to give battle. As Ferguson was the only British soldier there, it was a contest between two groups of Americans. Despite bayonet charges to drive off the attackers who surrounded them, the defenders were whittled down, and when Ferguson was killed, the survivors tried to surrender. Many of these men were shot down by the patriots before the militia officers could restore order. While the loyalists lost their entire force (400 killed, and 600 taken prisoner), patriot casualties were negligible. Further reprisal killings continued as the prisoners were led away to the north. Cornwallis had not only lost an able commander, but his flank was left wide open. Appalled at the disaster, he called off his invasion and led his troops back to the security of Winnsboro.

On 14 October, on the same day that Cornwallis learned of the disaster at King's Mountain, General Washington appointed a new commander to replace the disgraced General Gates. His choice was Major-General Nathaniel Greene, a tall, stocky, self-educated 38-year-old from Rhode Island. Greene was something of a protégé of Washington's, and his experience as the Quartermaster General to the army during the winter it spent in Valley Forge would stand him in good stead in the Carolinas. On 3 December 1780, Greene rode into the army's winter encampment at Charlotte and took command of the American army in the south. What he found was alarming, as sickness and desertion had whittled his force of regulars down to less than 800 men out of a muster strength of 2,307. The

The port of Charleston, South Carolina, served as the initial objective for Sir Henry Clinton's renewed offensive in the southern colonies, and acted as the principal British base for the ensuing campaign.

Major-General Horatio Gates (1728–1806) was known as 'the hero of Saratoga', and great things were expected of him when he took command of American forces in the south after the fall of Charleston. Instead, he threw away his army at Camden (1780), and ruined his career by fleeing from the field.

21

RIGHT Irregular militia in the Carolinas continued to harry British outposts and supply lines despite the setbacks inflicted on American conventional forces in the region. This scene purports to depict Francis Marion and some of his followers.

BELOW The battle of King's Mountain (1780) was fought on these steep, tree-clad slopes. The "over-the-mountain men" climbed the hill, and despite repeated bayonet charges by the loyalist defenders, they managed to gain the summit and overrun the defenders' position.

militia he needed to bolster his regulars had returned to their homes, and diplomacy was required to encourage them to rejoin the army. Similarly, Greene's logistical skills were tested as he sought to reprovision his dispirited and poorly equipped troops. By the middle of December, the local supplies of food had become depleted, so foraging parties had to travel further afield. Greene moved his army to Cheraw on the Peedee River, where supplies were more abundant. To keep Cornwallis occupied, he detached a force of Continental Line, his cavalry and some militia to operate in the South Carolina "backcountry" north of the line of British outposts. The force was commanded by Brigadier-General Daniel Morgan, whose orders were to rendezvous with local patriot forces and harry the British. As Greene put it: "He cannot leave Morgan behind him to come at me, or his outposts of Ninety-Six and Augusta would be exposed … and he cannot chase Morgan far or prosecute his views upon Virginia, while I am here with the whole country open before me. I am as near Charleston as he is." Greene was quite correct. In order to counter the threat posed by Morgan, Cornwallis had to divide his army, and send a fast-moving striking force to the north. The man he chose to lead this important column was his dashing cavalry commander, Lieutenant-Colonel Banastre Tarleton.

Tarleton commanded his own British Legion, supported by two British line battalions, some light infantry and a detachment of light guns. In all, he commanded 1,100 men, while Morgan could muster 1,000 men, including 400 regulars. Tarleton rode out of Winnsbro on 6 January, while Cornwallis advanced his army up the banks of the Broad River some 40 miles to Turkey Creek, where he could provide support if anything went wrong. Further reinforcements (1,500 men commanded by Major-General Leslie) were summoned from Virginia to reinforce the

The death of Major Patrick Ferguson at King's Mountain (1780) was a grievous blow to the British cause in the southern campaign. Although over 1,000 men a side fought in the battle, Ferguson was the only regular soldier among them.

RIGHT **Following their victory at King's Mountain the patriot forces exacted revenge on their loyalist opponents. Several were hanged following a hearing by a "kangaroo court." One bitter patriot observer exclaimed, "Would to God every tree in the wilderness bore such fruit as that."**

BELOW **The battlefield of Cowpens, viewed from the American main line of positions. The openness of the terrain is illusory, as Morgan used small folds in the ground to conceal his second and third line from Tarleton's troops.**

ABOVE **The grave of Major Patrick Ferguson on the lower slopes of King's Mountain, South Carolina. He refused to surrender "to such a damned banditti," and was shot from his saddle during the closing moments of the battle.**

ABOVE, LEFT **In this dramatic but hopelessly inaccurate early 19th-century depiction of the battle of Cowpens, Morgan is shown leading his Continental Line forward in a counter-charge, while the British begin to flee the field. In fact, the 71st Highlanders stood their ground until it became apparent that further resistance could only result in a needless slaughter.**

main army. Morgan's men had advanced as far south as the Saluda River, but in the face of Tarleton's advance they retreated north towards the fords over the Broad River south of Gilbert Town. When Morgan discovered the fords were swollen by rain and that Tarleton was only ten miles away, he turned to give battle. He chose to fight on the Cowpens, a stretch of pastureland and woodland that looked deceptively open. His skilful deployment in three ranks meant that his front line of riflemen and militia would have to take the full weight of Tarleton's attack. He ordered them to fire three shots, then to retire to the rear. His second line of militia had similar orders, while his third line of veteran regulars had orders to hold fast. The two small armies met soon after dawn on 17 January 1781. True to form, Tarleton ordered an immediate attack, his infantry deployed in the centre and the cavalry divided between his flanks. The riflemen of the first American line caused a heavy toll, as did the second line. By the time the British reached the third line of regulars, the disciplined fire of the Maryland and Delaware regulars halted the British advance. At that moment Morgan unleashed his cavalry reserve into the fight, and his militia, who had regrouped,

LEFT **In this early representation of the battle of Cowpens (1781), Morgan is shown advancing, while Tarleton (on the left) is shown riding away from the Americans. The accuracy of the depiction can be gauged by the inclusion of an American Indian in the foreground, scalping a redcoat!**

ABOVE **Brigadier-General Daniel Morgan (1736–1802) won a brilliant victory at Cowpens in January 1781, but a serious case of sciatica prevented him from taking a more active part in the ensuing Guilford Courthouse campaign.**

RIGHT **The reverse of the "Cowpens Medal" depicts Brigadier-General Morgan in a detail from the popular woodcut of the battle. The medal was awarded to Morgan and his officers by a grateful Congress a year after the battle.**

returned to the fight. Charged in their front and in both flanks, the British line wavered, then broke, the retreat being led by the cavalrymen of the British Legion. Tarleton tried to break the American cavalry, but it was too late, and he was forced to quit the field. With over 300 men dead and 525 taken prisoner, Tarleton's command was virtually destroyed. The stunning American victory left Cornwallis with barely 1,000 men. The loss of so many regular troops was a bitter blow, and when Tarleton and the remnants of his army limped into the camp at Turkey Creek the day after the battle, Cornwallis was determined to have his revenge. The stage was set for the dramatic pursuit of the American army, a campaign that would result in the clash at Guilford Courthouse less than two months later.

OPPOSING COMMANDERS

BRITISH

Lieutenant-General Charles, Earl Cornwallis (1738–1805) commanded the British army that fought at Guilford Courthouse, and despite his historical legacy as "the man who lost at Yorktown," he was probably the most gifted field commander in the British army during the war. He left Eton to join the Guards in 1756, and fought his first battle at Minden three years later. Following this action he became a captain, was elected to Parliament in 1760, and subsequently promoted to lieutenant-colonel and named the commander of the 12th Foot. Having seen action in Germany, in 1762 he became the second Earl Cornwallis on the death of his father. Support at court helped win him promotion to colonel of the 33rd Foot three years later, and he was also named Constable of the Tower of London in 1770. Following the revolt of the colonies, he was promoted to major-general, and in early 1776 he sailed for America. During the battles around New York in 1776 he displayed considerable flair for battlefield command, and his actions led to a crushing British victory, and the capture of the city. He allowed himself to be outmanoeuvred by Washington during the Trenton campaign of 1776–77, earning the scathing criticism of General Howe, the first of two senior commanders he would fall out with. He recovered his reputation during the fighting around Philadelphia in 1777–78, and in particular his performance at the battles of Brandywine (1777) and Monmouth (1778) demonstrated his martial prowess to both his superiors and his men. In the aftermath of General Clinton's capture of Charleston in 1780, Cornwallis was left to bring the campaign in the Carolinas to a successful conclusion. He demonstrated great skill at the battle of Camden (1780), but fell foul of Clinton, and a rancour developed that would hinder British prosecution of the war. Following the twin defeats of British columns at King's Mountain (1780) and Cowpens (1781), Cornwallis vowed revenge, and decided to pursue the American forces of Generals Morgan and Greene. The result was the Guilford Courthouse campaign. Although criticized for squandering his army in the battle to no good effect, he outfought his opponents, only to make the error of leaving the Carolinas virtually undefended while he took the war into Virginia. His subsequent defeat at Yorktown marked the end of the active British prosecution of the war, and marked the nadir of Cornwallis's military fortunes. After the war he went on to serve in India where, once again, he re-established his reputation as one of Britain's best field commanders. Yet his skills in the field were flawed by strategic shortcomings. Cornwallis has been described as "an English aristocrat of the finest type…", an "example of antique and singleminded patriotism." These virtues were not enough, however, to triumph in the struggle for the southern colonies.

Major-General Sir Alexander Leslie (1740–94) was the Scottish-born commander of the 64th Foot when the American colonies revolted, and while still a lieutenant-colonel he was ordered to Boston, then New York, where he was given command of a light infantry brigade. His performance at the battle of White Plains and during the Trenton campaign (1776) was lacklustre. He was one of the few senior commanders available in the Americas, however, so in 1780 he was duly promoted. He took command of a force charged with carrying out a diversionary attack on the Chesapeake Bay tidewater, while Clinton launched his army against Charleston. He then joined Cornwallis's army in time to participate in the "Race to the Dan." He narrowly escaped drowning during the skirmish at Cowan's Ford, but performed well during the pursuit of Greene's army. During the battle of Guilford Courthouse Leslie commanded the right wing of the British army with competence but not flair, and his inability to control his forces more closely allowed his wing of the army to become divided into two unsupported groups as the battle progressed. After the battle Cornwallis sent him back to Charleston "for health reasons," and although he succeeded Cornwallis as commander of the southern theatre after Yorktown (1781), his uninspiring performance led to the eventual evacuation of the Carolinas in December 1782.

The illegitimate son of Lord Trawley, **Colonel Charles O'Hara (c.1740–1802)** commanded the two Guards battalions at Guilford Courthouse. He entered the army in 1752, and four years later he joined the Coldstream Guards, his father's regiment. His army career involved service in both Europe and Africa, and he became a lieutenant-colonel of his regiment in 1769. O'Hara and the Guards arrived in the Americas in 1778. The following year he was made a brevet colonel, and given command of the Guards Brigade of two battalions. This promotion came in time for him to see service in the southern colonies, and his force acted as the mainstay of Cornwallis's army during the "Race to the Dan" and the subsequent Guilford Courthouse campaign. He proved a valuable asset to his commander-in-chief, particularly during the crossing of Cowan's Ford on 1 February 1781, and at Guilford Courthouse, when he rallied the Guards for a second attack on the American third line, despite being wounded during the action. His Guardsmen broke the back of American resistance, and forced General Greene's army to quit the field. This gifted commander continued to serve in Cornwallis's army until the denouement at Yorktown, where he represented his Commander-in-Chief during the surrender ceremony.

Lieutenant-Colonel Banastre Tarleton (1754–1833) has been vilified as what today would be termed a "war criminal," but his conduct was no worse than many independent commanders on both sides. Both the loyalist and patriot civilian populations in the Carolinas suffered repressive measures at the hands of their enemies. Born in Liverpool, Tarleton joined the King's (1st) Dragoon Guards as a cornet in 1775 and then volunteered for service in America. Although he reached America in mid-1776, he only began to make a name for himself six months later when, as the commander of a detachment of light dragoons, he captured General Lee, Washington's most senior subordinate. By 1778 Captain Tarleton was appointed lieu-

Major-General Alexander Leslie (1740–94) was ordered to reinforce Cornwallis's army with troops from Virginia. He and his men arrived in Cornwallis's camp on the same day as Tarleton and his survivors limped in after escaping from the debacle at Cowpens. (Private Collection)

Lieutenant-Colonel Banastre Tarleton (1754–1833) was Cornwallis's dashing and impetuous cavalry commander. He earned a probably unwarranted reputation for ruthlessness, but his greatest fault was his reckless nature, a failing that led to his defeat at Cowpens in January 1781. (National Gallery, London)

tenant-colonel, and he was given command of a force of provincial cavalry, the British Legion. This loyalist force accompanied the army during the southern campaign, and Tarleton quickly made a name for himself as a gifted cavalry commander, raiding enemy outposts and scouting ahead of the main army. His tactics also earned him the nickname "Bloody Tarleton" from his patriot opponents. On 17 January 1781 his fast-moving force of cavalry, foot and artillery was defeated by General Morgan at the battle of Cowpens, setting into motion the train of events that would lead to Guilford Courthouse. To many British regulars, Tarleton's defeat highlighted his lack of military experience and demonstrated his tendency to act impulsively. Despite this, he remained a valuable cavalry commander, and he served with distinction during the Guilford Courthouse campaign, being wounded during the final stages of the battle on 15 March 1781.

Lieutenant-Colonel James Webster (1743–81) commanded the left wing of the British army at Guilford Courthouse. The son of an Edinburgh minister, he became a lieutenant in the 33rd Foot in 1760, and by the time the regiment was sent to the Americas in 1776, Webster was its commander. As the 33rd was Lord Cornwallis's old regiment it tended to be attached to his command, and Webster and his commander-in-chief developed a strong working relationship. His ability as a battlefield commander was demonstrated during the battle of Monmouth (1778), and within a year he was given command of a brigade, consisting of his own regiment and the 23rd Fusiliers. He sailed south with his brigade, which had a composite light-infantry battalion attached. This force participated in the attack on Charleston and the battle of Camden (1780), then formed part of Cornwallis's force during the Guilford Courthouse campaign. Webster performed well at Weitzel's Mill (6 March 1781), and at Guilford Courthouse. He was mortally wounded during the attack on the American third line, and died two weeks after the battle. Tarleton wrote of Webster that he, "united all the virtues of civil life with the gallantry and professional knowledge of a soldier." This tough, experienced Scotsman was one of Cornwallis's most gifted commanders, and his loss was a grievous blow to his commander, and was probably a contributory factor to the ultimate failure of Cornwallis's southern campaign.

AMERICAN

Major-General Nathaniel Greene (1742–86) lost the battle of Guilford Courthouse, but he emerged from the campaign with a shining reputation, second only to that of his commander-in-chief, George Washington. He was brought up in Rhode Island as a Quaker, but his preoccupation with military matters led to him being ostracized by his Quaker community. He raised a company of militia, and in 1775 he was named as a brigadier of militia. He was then appointed to command a brigade of the Continental Army. Although illness kept him from his duties during the New York campaign of 1776, shortly after his promotion to major-general the forces at his command were badly defeated at Fort Washington. His reputation was restored during the Trenton campaign, but he was criticized for his growing influence with Washington, and for his own stormy relationship with the Continental Congress. After commanding a

Major-General Nathaniel Greene (1742–86) was an inspired choice as the new commander of American forces in the southern theatre. His administrative and logistical skills were vital to ensure his American army recovered from its reverses, and his tactical and strategic abilities were both highly developed. (Independence National Historical Park, Valley Forge, Pennsylvania)

wing of the army at Brandywine and Germantown, his performance as quartermaster-general at Valley Forge did much to save the American army during the winter of 1777/78. Following a brief return to active command during the Monmouth and Newport campaigns of 1778, Greene resumed his administrative duties during the winter of 1778/79. Stung by Congressional criticism of his financial interests and by claims of favouritism, he resigned his post, and Washington sent him to West Point, to keep an eye on the British garrison in New York. The defeat of General Gates at Camden (16 August 1780) gave Washington the opportunity to send his protégé to restore the situation in the south. The resulting campaigns would prove to be amongst the most successful American operations of the war. His reliance on Brigadier-General Daniel Morgan to goad the British was inspired, and during the "Race to the Dan" that followed he not only outmanoeuvred Cornwallis, but also held his army together. His performance at Guilford Courthouse made the best possible use of the forces under his command, and it was only the determination of Cornwallis and the professionalism of his troops that resulted in a British victory. Greene went on to spearhead the reconquest of South Carolina. Although defeated tactically at Guilford Courthouse, he proved the strategic victor of the campaign.

Colonel William Washington (1752–1810) was a kinsman of the American commander-in-chief, and the leader of Greene's small cavalry arm. When the revolt began he was studying to become a cleric, but he abandoned his theological studies to become a captain in the 3rd Virginia Continentals. Following his actions during the New York and Trenton campaigns of 1776, he was promoted to the rank of major, and transferred to the cavalry. Within a year he had become the lieutenant-colonel of the 3rd Continental Dragoons. He fought in defence of Charleston (1780), but his cavalry was defeated by Tarleton's British Legion. For the rest of the year he led cavalry raids against Cornwallis's outposts, and fought with distinction at Cowpens (1781). During the subsequent Guilford Courthouse campaign Washington behaved as a light-cavalry commander should, screening his own army while harassing the enemy. His cavalry charge at Guilford Courthouse almost turned the tide of battle, and following the engagement Washington went on to enjoy further successes in South Carolina.

The commander of Lee's Legion was **Lieutenant-Colonel Henry "Light Horse Harry" Lee (1756–1818)**, a courageous and energetic officer. In 1776 he was made a captain of Virginia cavalry, and he fought so well during the Philadelphia Campaign (1777) that he was promoted and given the opportunity to expand his command into a mixed force of horse and foot. Dubbed "Lee's Partisan Corps" but later renamed "Lee's Legion", this force was sent south to join General Greene's army in late 1780. He helped screen Greene during the "Race to the Dan," and then fought at Guilford Courthouse. Although criticized for his failure to remain in contact with Greene's army, his troops tied down powerful units of the British army that could have been deployed more effectively in the main engagement against Greene's veteran third line.

General Edward Stevens (1745–1820) commanded the Virginia militia that tipped the strategic balance, and gave Greene the opportunity to

TOP **Colonel William Washington (1752–1810) commanded the regular cavalry component of Greene's army with skill and daring. He played a decisive part in the American victory at Cowpens, and his charge at Guilford Courthouse almost altered the outcome of the battle. (Independence National Historical Park, Valley Forge, Pennsylvania)**

ABOVE **Lieutenant-Colonel Henry "Light Horse Harry" Lee (1756–1818) commanded Lee's Legion, a mixed force of both dragoons and infantry. During the battle of Guilford Courthouse his troops fought against the Hessian von Bose Regiment and elements of the Foot Guards. (Independence National Historical Park, Valley Forge, Pennsylvania)**

Colonel Otho Holland Williams (1749–94) fought at the battle of Camden (1780), then led the same Maryland regulars during the Guilford Courthouse campaign. He was given command of Greene's rearguard during the later stages of the "Race to the Dan". (Independence National Historical Park, Valley Forge, Pennsylvania)

Colonel John Eager Howard (1752–1827) distinguished himself at Cowpens (1781), then took command of the 1st Maryland Regiment during the closing stages of the battle of Guilford Courthouse, and his actions helped preserve Greene's army. (Independence National Historical Park, Valley Forge, Pennsylvania)

fight it out with Cornwallis's British regulars. Born in Culpeper County, Virginia, he commanded a militia battalion in 1775 before being promoted to colonel and given command of a Virginia regiment in the Continental Army. He fought in all the main battles of the Philadelphia Campaign (1777) but then resigned his commission to serve as a militia commander in his home state. Although his brigade of Virginia militiamen performed disgracefully at the battle of Camden (1780), Stevens displayed courage and resourcefulness, and was given a second chance. His men formed the second line at Guilford Courthouse, and this time they stood long enough to inflict heavy casualties on the enemy before retiring. Stevens was badly wounded in the battle, but he recovered in time to be present at the surrender of Cornwallis at Yorktown. He went on to become a state senator.

Brigadier-General Isaac Huger (1743–1797) was a native of South Carolina, one of five brothers who served the American cause during the war. He first saw action in the state militia during its war against the Cherokee Indians (1760). He was named lieutenant-colonel of the 1st South Carolina Regiment in 1775, and by 1778 he had risen to the rank of brigadier-general. He was severely wounded during an engagement near Charleston (1779), and continued to serve in South Carolina during the Charleston campaign where he was bested by Tarleton. During the Guilford Courthouse campaign he commanded a brigade of Virginian regulars, and was again badly wounded. He recovered in time to serve in Greene's invasion of South Carolina the following month, performing his duties with distinction and courage yet again.

One of the most experienced officers in the Continental Army, **Colonel Otho Holland Williams (1749–94)** commanded a brigade of two Maryland regiments at Guilford Courthouse. Born in Maryland to Welsh parents, Williams worked as a clerk before embarking on a commercial career in 1774. The following year, when war erupted, he became a lieutenant in a company of Maryland riflemen, and joined the American army outside Boston. The following year he was promoted to major, then took command of his regiment following the death of its commanding officer. He was wounded and captured at Fort Washington, NY, and he remained incarcerated until early 1778, when he was released due to his ill health. While he was held prisoner he had been promoted to colonel, and so on his release he was given command of the 6th Maryland Regiment of the Continental Army, which he led into battle at Monmouth on 28 June 1778. In April 1780 he was sent south to form part of General Gates' American army. Although the army was defeated at Camden (1780), Williams fought well, and Gates' successor General Greene recognized his abilities. He was given command of a corps of light troops which screened the forces of Greene and Morgan during the "Race to the Dan" following the battle of Cowpens (1781). During the Guilford Courthouse campaign he performed brilliantly, and went on to lead his Continental Army brigade back into South Carolina to avenge his defeat at Camden. An exceptional brigade commander, Williams was of inestimable value to Greene.

OPPOSING ARMIES

THE BRITISH

The troops available to Lieutenant-General Cornwallis included some of the finest soldiers in the British army. Despite setbacks in other theatres of the war, these men had a consummate and well-founded belief in their own professional abilities, and their military experience made them veterans. His army was a small one – a mere six regiments of regular infantry, supported by a detachment of Royal Artillery and the loyalist American dragoons of the British Legion. Regardless of their numbers, they engaged and defeated an American army twice their size, and held the blood-soaked field of battle. There can be no greater testimony to the professionalism of the British "redcoat" than the accomplishment of this feat of arms, albeit one which cost the British dear.

The five regiments of British infantry were the core of the army. They consisted of the 1st and 2nd battalions of the Foot Guards, the 23rd and 33rd Regiments of Foot, and the 2nd Battalion of the 71st (Highland) Regiment of Foot, a unit that was usually referred to as Fraser's

Musket Drill, from the *Manual Exercise of the Foot Guards* (1761), a tactical manual which was reprinted on both sides of the Atlantic during the American Revolutionary period. It demonstrated the complex evolutions demanded of well-trained regular infantry.

LEFT "Soldiers of the British Army in the Americas," from an early 19th-century representation. Apart from the hussar, the depictions of dress and equipment are reasonably accurate.

Highlanders. Most regiments in the army consisted of a single battalion, but both the Regiment of Foot Guards and the 71st Highlanders were exceptions to this rule. The 71st boasted two battalions, while the Foot Guards consisted of seven battalions. As the latter were regarded as the personal troops of His Majesty King George III, their primary duty being the protection the monarch, only the King himself could grant permission for service overseas.

On paper at least, each battalion consisted of some 674 men including 25 officers, a surgeon and his assistant and a chaplain. These men were divided into ten companies. In 1775 the army approved the raising of two additional companies per regiment, but the change was never put into practice. One of the ten companies was designated a grenadier company, and consisted of the tallest and strongest men in the regiment, while a light infantry company was made up of the regiment's best marksmen. Together, these two companies were designated "flank companies," as opposed to "battalion companies," and were usually placed on the right and left of the regimental line respectively. The flank companies of several regiments were often detached, then amalgamated into ad-hoc formations of either grenadiers or light infantry, a practice that Cornwallis employed at Guilford Courthouse. In theory, every company consisted of 67 men, including three officers, but their actual strength seldom matched this "paper" strength. Although each company nominally included 56 privates, each company was allowed three "contingent men" on their rolls, an accounting exercise that enabled the pay for three privates to be allocated to company funds. These contingent men were a fiction. In addition, regimental strengths were always well below their allotted paper strength, and companies of 20–30 men were typical in Cornwallis's army. Each battalion was commanded by a lieutenant-colonel with a major acting as second-in-command. In theory, both these officers commanded companies, but in practice their companies were led by junior officers, leaving the senior men to command the regiment itself. Commanded by a Captain, assisted by a lieutenant and an ensign, each company also included three sergeants and three corporals and two drummers or fifers – four for the Grenadier company.

While the last army returns were filed two weeks before the battle and, therefore, we do not know the precise number of men in each unit, these returns do provide an approximation of the number of infantry available to Cornwallis on the morning of the battle. The eight battalion companies of the two battalions of Foot Guards consisted of approximately 200–250 men each, while the two combined companies of light infantrymen totalled 100 men. The Guards' two combined grenadier companies were kept close to full strength by drafts from the battalion companies, so 120 grenadiers from the Guards fought at Guilford Courthouse. Almost half of the British redcoats who fought in the battle were, therefore, elite soldiers of the Foot Guards. The 33rd Regiment of Foot was formerly Cornwallis's regiment, and had fought in the Americas since the summer of 1776. It listed 322 men on its rolls, but this total includes men unavailable or unfit for duty, such as the sick and wounded. The 23rd Regiment of Foot was a fusilier formation and as such they were regarded as a "royal" regiment (in this case the Royal Welsh Fusiliers) and something of an elite unit. In reality, both the veterans of the 23rd and the 33rd Foot were veteran troops. The Fusiliers listed 258 men on their rolls, including those unfit for duty. From the statistical evidence provided by Cornwallis's other returns we can assume that as many as a third of these men were not fit for duty on 15 March 1781, reducing the effective strength of the 23rd and 33rd Foot to approximately 170 and 215 men respectively. The 71st Foot (Fraser's Highlanders) mustered a mere 212 men, or 140 men if their strength is adjusted to allow for sick and unfit men. The field strength of Cornwallis's regiments thus bore little relation to the theoretical "paper" strengths and demonstrate the effects of the hard campaigning these units had already seen in the Americas.

The backbone of the British army was the "redcoat"; a tough, professional soldier whose service in the army was regarded as one step above penal servitude. On enlistment, service was set at three years, but this could be (and was) extended to the end of the war. Recruits were meant to measure at least 5ft 6in. in height, be of the Protestant faith, and be aged between 17 and 30. In reality, the war proved unpopular in Britain, and as recruiting levels were low, such restrictions were often waived. Although he served in a particular regiment, a soldier could be transferred from its ranks into another formation at the whim of his commanding officer. He was also subject to the harsh discipline of the army's articles of war, which gave officers and their non-commissioned subordinates extensive powers over the men in their charge. Even minor infractions could be punished by harsh discipline, flogging, or even summary execution. Soldiers endured all this for a mere eightpence a day. Of this, a third was retained by the army to pay for clothing, and up to

The uniform of the British grenadier changed immediately before the war. The older style of mitre shown here was replaced by a more imposing but equally impractical fur version. At Guilford Courthouse the British grenadier companies of the Guards were combined into a single unit.

RIGHT In this contemporary cartoon depicting a Hessian grenadier the artist captured the heavy burden that these troops were expected to carry on campaign. Their packs were usually removed and stacked before the troops went into battle.

An American soldier of the Continental Line. Supply problems and atrocious campaigning conditions meant that the infantry in Greene's army would never have looked as well attired as this.

fivepence could be used to cover the provision of sustenance. In effect, the average redcoat rarely saw much of his pay.

The redcoat derived his nickname from his uniform, a brick-red woollen surcoat, the lapels and cuffs of which were turned back to form facings in an approved regimental colour (blue for the Guards and Fusiliers, red for the 33rd and white for the Highlanders). Beneath it a short, sleeveless waistcoat was worn; white for most troops, red for light infantry. Close-fitting white trousers with black calf-length gaiters completed the official dress, along with a black felt tricorne hat and black shoes. The grenadiers and the light infantrymen of each regiment wore their own distinctive caps, as did the fusiliers. In theory at least, the Highlanders wore kilts in the government tartan, and sported blue highland bonnets. Many of these uniforms were adapted to better suit the conditions in the field. For the Highlanders this meant that their kilts were replaced with trousers, while regulation white trousers were often replaced with ones cut from any available brown or unbleached cloth. Although the grenadiers still retained their distinctive mitres, there is evidence that the light infantry and many of the men of the battalion companies of the British foot regiments wore black felt round hats, many of which were cut down from the issue tricorne. A wide belt was worn over the left shoulder from which was suspended a 60-round cartridge box. Grenadiers also carried a hanger (a small sword) on the same belt. A knapsack, haversack and blanket further encumbered the redcoat. Including his rifle and a bayonet hung from his waistbelt, the average redcoat carried a total of 60lbs of equipment. Before battle all non-essential equipment would be removed, hopefully to be collected after the action.

Each redcoat carried a Long Land Pattern Musket, a design that was first introduced in 1715 under the supervision of the Duke of Marlborough. A more familiar name for the weapon was the "Brown Bess," although the term was only first used in print in 1781. Several variants of the basic design were introduced in the intervening half-century since its introduction, but all versions of the weapon shared certain characteristics. The bore was 0.75in., which allowed a 1¼-ounce lead ball to be fired from it. The barrel length was 46in., although the Short Land Pattern musket introduced in 1768 had a shorter barrel of 42in., but most existing muskets were shortened by sawing four inches from the barrel. The total weight of the piece was a little over 12lbs. These were flintlock weapons, and although reliable, they were far from accurate. Major George Hanger of the British Legion wrote that: "a soldier's musket, if not exceedingly ill-bored … will strike the figure of a man at eighty yards; it may even at 100; but a soldier must be very unfortunate indeed who shall be wounded … at 150 yards, provided his antagonist aims at him…. I do main [-tain] … that no man was ever killed at 200 yards by a common soldier's musket, by the person who aimed at him."

As recruitment into the army was a continual problem for the British, in late 1775 negotiations were opened with several small German states for the supply of mercenary troops for service in America. Two such formations were present in Cornwallis's army. The Von Bose Regiment was a battalion-sized formation from Hesse-Cassel in central Germany. It consisted of 353 men (including sick and wounded) in five companies. Unlike the British, these Hessians wore dark coats. In order to help offset

Hessian troops on the march. Unlike many armies during the war, Cornwallis's column was not burdened by a swarm of camp followers, including women and children. Rather it was Greene's troops who were hampered by refugees and families as they tried to escape the British.

the apparent tactical advantage conferred on the Americans by their riflemen, units of rifle-armed German Jägers were recruited for service in America. Eighty-four of these green-coated light infantry served with Cornwallis.

The two remaining elements of the British army at Guilford Courthouse were the artillery and cavalry arms. Cornwallis had three field guns at his disposal, all 3-pdrs, whose 42in. long brass barrels were mounted on light "galloper" carriages, making them highly mobile weapons. They were equipped to fire both roundshot and canister, the latter being used as a close-range, anti-personnel round that effectively turned the cannon into a large shotgun.

The final unit in the army was the British Legion, a mixed force of loyalist horse and foot numbering 274 men. Of these, approximately half were mounted, while the remainder of the green-coated Legion served as infantry. Although Tarleton's loyalists lacked the élan they enjoyed before their defeat at Cowpens, they were still an experienced and battle-hardened unit, capable of countering the threat posed by Greene's American cavalry.

In total, Cornwallis had just over 2,000 men under his command and ready to give battle on the morning of 15 March 1781. Although they faced twice their number of American opponents, Cornwallis could rely on the greater discipline and experience of his regulars to offset the American numerical advantage.

THE AMERICANS

When George Washington sent General Nathaniel Greene south to succeed the disgraced General Horatio Gates in August 1780, the new commander did not know in what condition he would find his defeated army. He knew the nucleus of regular regiments survived, but they lacked even the most basic supplies of food, clothing and equipment. When he arrived at the army's headquarters in Charlotte, North Carolina, that December, he found the situation was far worse than expected. Of the 2,400 regular troops under his command, only a third were fit for duty. As Greene wrote, he inherited "but the shadow of an army in the midst of distress." It is a testimony to Greene's skills as a military administrator that in just over six months he transformed this force into an army capable of facing the British in battle and beating them.

The core of Greene's force were the veteran regiments of the Continental Army. When the American Revolution began, all the forces available to General George Washington were militiamen. By the late spring of 1775, the Second Continental Congress approved the formation of a standing army, which was initially dubbed the New England army. By the summer it had become known as the "Continental Army" and its units as the "Continental Line." Although Congress was initially reluctant to sanction the creation of a standing army for longer than a year, the reverses of 1776 prompted them to allow Washington to "take direction of affairs," and approved the army's continued existence until the end of the war. Soldiers were given the opportunity to re-enlist, but few chose to do so, as service in the militia of their home state proved a preferable option. Recruitment resulted in the inclusion of "vagabonds and strollers" as well as eager volunteers, but by 1777 the first flush of revolutionary fervour had passed, and the army was hard-pressed to maintain a flow of recruits into the ranks. As Washington put it in 1778, "the country had been already pretty well drained of that class of men whose tempers, attachments and circumstances disposed them to enter permanently … into the army." By mid-1778 the majority of these regiments were organized into eight companies, plus an additional light company, although ten-company regiments were also common. The paper strength of a company varied depending on the unit's home state, but the Virginia and Maryland regiments had a full complement of 50 men, including three officers, six non-commissioned officers and two musicians. Like the British, the units that fought at Guilford Courthouse were all understrength, and the four Continental Line regiments present (4th and 5th Virginia, 1st and 2nd Maryland) fielded no more than 360–400 men apiece. The Virginia regiments were slightly stronger than their counterparts from Maryland, due to the proximity of their recruiting centres. In addition, the understrength Delaware infantry (augmented by a company of Virginians) could only muster 110 men who acted as light infantry. Of these regular troops the 1st Maryland and the Delaware regiments contained some of the best soldiers in either army, and were battle-hardened, well led and highly motivated.

These troops were trained to fight in the standard linear fashion of the period, just like their British opponents. This meant they deployed in two or three ranks, the men standing shoulder to shoulder in a battle line. The formation allowed for the greatest concentration of firepower, and most units were trained to provide a continuous fire by sections or companies, or to deliver crushing massed volleys. In action the unit would fire when their target advanced to within 75–100 yards, or on occasion hold their fire until the enemy closed to 50 yards. At this virtually point-blank range, the infantry would deliver a series of volleys, and weight of fire was deemed more important than accuracy. If both sides withstood these exchanges, one might consider closing with the

ABOVE **Of all the depictions of infantrymen of the period, this representation of a ragged American soldier is probably one of the more accurate. By the time Greene's men crossed the Dan River into Virginia, their uniforms were ragged, and many soldiers had no shoes.**

ABOVE, RIGHT **"Baron" Friedrich Wilhelm von Steuben (1730–94) drilling his troops at Valley Forge, Pennsylvania. As Inspector General of the Continental Army, this Prussian soldier was instrumental in turning the regular American army into an efficient fighting force, capable of meeting the British redcoats in battle.**

bayonet. By this stage in the war, the best of the Continental Line were capable of meeting the finest regiments of the British army or their mercenary allies on equal terms.

Virginia and North Carolina Militia

The bulk of General Greene's army were less reliable. These were the state militias of Virginia and North Carolina, a force composed of regiments formed locally in towns, counties and districts. They were intended for home defence rather than for regular service, and as such they usually lacked the training and battle experience of regular troops. First raised to fight the Indians or the French, the American militia

RIGHT **An American rifleman. Two rifle units of Carolinian militia were present at the battle of Guilford Courthouse, on the extreme flanks of the first defensive line. Although they had a slow rate of fire, these rifles were capable of hitting targets at ranges in excess of 250 yards.**

Troopers of Lee's Legion. While his infantry wore purple coats, the cavalry tunics were green, making them similar in appearance to the troopers of Tarleton's British Legion. This similarity was exploited during the campaign by "Light Horse Harry" Lee.

An American light infantryman from the light infantry company of a Continental Line regiment. These troops wore a distinctive short cap, and were trained to fight both as part of a firing line or as skirmishers. They were armed with shorter "fusil" versions of the standard Charleville musket.

system was adapted and expanded during the War of Independence. By 1781, most militiamen had never fired a musket in anger, while experienced frontiersmen were usually grouped into special militia rifle units. Two such battalions of Virginian riflemen were present at Guilford Courthouse, each containing four companies of approximately 50 men each. Unlike the regular militia, who were trained to fire in ranks, they relied on close-range musketry. Although the riflemen were highly effective, and could hit targets at 250 yards, they were vulnerable if the enemy closed to contact with them as they lacked any bayonets with which to defend themselves. The same could be said of the militia, who were rarely issued with precious bayonets.

Initially, George Washington had a low opinion of militia, stating: "To place any dependence on Militia is assuredly resting upon a broken reed." Unfortunately, without them, Greene would have been unable to face the British. The performance of southern militia regiments led to the debacle at Camden (1780), but it can be argued that too much was expected of them, and if used by a commander who understood these men, they could provide a useful addition to the army. One such leader was Brigadier-General Daniel Morgan, who at the battle of Cowpens

An American militiaman at the plough, in a print by Felix Darley. When a county was under threat, local militia were expected to be ready to fight at a moment's notice. The rapidity with which Greene could raise local militia during the "Race to the Dan" demonstrated the effectiveness of this policy of preparedness.

In this evocative engraving by Felix Darley, a soldier of an American Continental Line regiment is shown priming the charge in his musket. Although the French Charleville musket issued to Greene's troops fired a smaller ball than its British equivalent, it had no corresponding advantage in range or accuracy.

asked his militiamen to fire three volleys and then retire. Greene relied on Morgan's example when he formulated his plans for the deployment of his army. His first line consisted of two Carolina militia brigades, containing approximately 500 men each, while the second line of Virginia militia was also grouped into two brigades, each of about 600 men. These latter formations were deemed to be particularly effective, as they contained a significant portion of time-expired Continental regulars.

The remainder of the American army consisted of an artillery detachment of 60 regular gunners of the 1st Continental Artillery, who crewed four 6-pdr guns, and a small but experienced cavalry arm. Of these, some 75 men formed the mounted element of Lee's Legion, supported by two companies of the Legion's light-infantry detachment. In addition, Colonel Washington commanded a force of approximately 86 cavalrymen of the 1st and 3rd Continental Dragoons. These two cavalry formations were valuable units, and would play a major part in the coming battle.

The Continental Army was forged into an effective fighting force at Valley Forge, Pennsylvania, during the harsh winter of 1777/78. Under the guidance of the Prussian "Baron" Friedrich von Steuben, who became Inspector General of the army in 1778, the Continental Line regiments adopted a set pattern of drill, marching and musketry, based loosely on the Prussian model. Under his guidance these soldiers of the American army transformed themselves into regular line infantry, capable of holding their own in a fight with the British redcoats.

In theory, these regulars of the Continental line were dressed in blue woollen surcoats, with red facings, white trousers and gaiters, a white vest or waistcoat, and a felt tricorne hat. In fact, supply problems necessitated the adoption of a variety of uniform types, including homemade hunting smocks and simple round hats or woollen caps. Many of Greene's supply problems improved during the weeks before the battle of Guilford Courthouse, and his regulars may have presented a more uniform appearance than previously. A crossbelt over the right shoulder supported a cartridge box, while the bayonet was carried on the left hip, together with a knapsack and a canteen. Like their British counterparts, these men carried a large smoothbore musket, a French weapon of the Charleville pattern that was similar in appearance to the British longarm.

THE CAMPAIGN

TO THE END OF THE WORLD – THE PURSUIT OF MORGAN

Before Cornwallis learned of the disaster that had befallen Tarleton, he was planning to renew his offensive into North Carolina. His objective was not to conquer territory, but to destroy Greene's army, or to drive it out of the Carolinas. On 18 January, having learned of the loss of over 800 men, he penned a despatch to his Commander-in-Chief, Sir Henry Clinton, in which he wrote: "Nothing but the most absolute necessity shall induce me to give up the important objective of the winter's campaign." His tiny army had just been reinforced by Major-General Leslie's 1,500 men: two battalions of the Foot Guards, the Hessian von Bose Regiment, and a detachment of German Jägers. His own troops encamped on Turkey Creek consisted of the 23rd and 33rd Regiments of Foot and the 2nd battalion of the 71st Highlanders, whose premier battalion had been destroyed at Cowpens. To this were added the survivors of Tarleton's command: 100 assorted infantry, 40 horsemen of the 17th Light Dragoons, and 200 loyalist dragoons of the British Legion. As the latter had fled the field, they were of dubious value until their morale was restored. Together, Cornwallis had 2,550 men at his disposal, a small but professional force, and more than a match for Greene and Morgan.

American militia receiving the call to arms. Although both patriots and loyalists made use of the tried-and-tested militia system in the Carolinas during the war, local militia were rarely a reliable military force on the battlefield, and they tended to return home if they considered they had served long enough.

During the "Race to the Dan," both armies marched northeast through the northern part of North Carolina during a period of heavy rain, which turned roads into quagmires and rivers into torrential barriers.

Although Morgan's men had a day's start, they might still be caught and destroyed and Cornwallis was determined to do so. The day after General Leslie's men arrived, Cornwallis ordered his men to break camp and march north. The loss of his cavalry and his lack of local loyalist support left him with practically no knowledge of the terrain in front of him. As a result, for two days he followed the wrong trail, leading towards Cowpens rather than due north. On 21 January he received intelligence that Morgan's small army was at Ramseur's Mill, some 30 miles to the north. He quickened the pace, and his men reached the mill on the evening of 24 January. By that time Morgan had moved on to the east, and was a day and a half's march ahead of his pursuers. Cornwallis's men were exhausted after six days of relentless forced marching along appalling roads. In order to allow his army to march more quickly, Cornwallis decided to burn his baggage train. Everything was destroyed, apart from the hospital wagons, his ammunition and salt. As one officer wrote, "Lord Cornwallis set the example by burning all his wagons, and destroying the greatest part of his baggage, which was followed by every officer of the army without a murmur." He also ordered his men to scour the countryside for food, and his men's shoes were repaired using a stock of leather found at the mill. After three days of rest, Cornwallis led his army east in pursuit of Morgan. O'Hara wrote: "In the most barren, inhospitable part of North America, opposed to the most savage, inveterate, perfidious, cruel enemy with zeal and bayonets only, it was resolved to follow Greene's army to the end of the world."

Morgan and his men crossed the Catawba River late on 23 January, and his men rested at Beattie's Ford while waiting for a reply to the message for help he had sent to General Greene at Cheraw. Morgan took the opportunity to hurry the prisoners captured at Cowpens to his rear, and with their escort they crossed the river at Island Ford on the upper reaches of the Catawba River, then took the road for Salisbury.

From Salisbury they continued into Virginia. Morgan set his men to watch the four fords over the Catawba. These were, from the north, Island's Ford, Sherill's Ford, Beattie's Ford and Cowan's Ford, each about five miles apart. On 30 January General Greene rode into Morgan's camp, and having just learned that Cornwallis had destroyed his own baggage train and seemed determined to pursue them, the two commanders discussed what to do next. They would attempt to stretch the British supply lines even further by continuing to retreat to the northeast. If the opportunity presented itself the Americans could then turn and fight Cornwallis at a time and on ground of their own choosing. For almost a week the Catawba had been in flood, rendering the fords impassable. On the last day of January the water levels began to fall and Greene ordered Morgan and his men to continue their retreat to Salisbury, where it was hoped they would be able to join forces with Greene's Continental Line under Brigadier-General Isaac Huger. Apart from his escort, the only troops remaining under Greene's command were the 800 local North Carolina militiamen of Rowan and Mecklenburg counties commanded by Brigadier-General Davidson. These men were to hold the Catawba fords for as long as possible then slip away to their homes. In the early afternoon Greene gave Morgan and Colonel Washington their instructions and then briefed General Davidson. While Greene retired several miles from the fords to rally more militia, Davidson deployed his men. He did not have enough men to contest every crossing, so Island Ford and Sherill's Ford were obstructed using felled trees and guarded by a small militia detachment. Five-hundred men defended the main crossing at Beattie's Ford while a further 300 held Cowan's Ford.

Cornwallis's army left their bivouac at Ramseur's Mill at dawn on 28 January and the following evening they made camp at Fawney's Plantation six miles west of the Catawba River. With his scouts reporting the river was too deep and fast flowing to cross he decided to wait for the waters to subside. By the evening of 31 January he deemed it just about safe enough to cross, and soon after midnight on 1 February the British

Soldiers make camp for the night. During the campaigning in the month preceding the battle, both sides marched and countermarched around the headwaters of the Haw River, and comfortable long-term encampments were rarely available.

broke camp and marched towards the river. Cornwallis correctly assumed that the bulk of Davidson's militia would be at Beattie's Ford, so he planned to outflank this main position with a surprise attack across Cowan's Ford five miles downstream to the south.

Lieutenant-Colonel Webster took the 33rd Foot and the artillery to pin the American force at Beattie's Ford, while Cornwallis sent the main force to Cowan's Ford. The river was about 500 yards wide at Cowan's Ford, and flowing very swiftly. Halfway across the river the ford split into two parts, with the main part stretching ahead known as Wagon Ford. The deeper Horse Ford branched off, reaching the eastern bank some 200 yards downstream.

Due to the fog that hung over the water, the militia sentries were unable to see the British advance guard plunge into the near-freezing water of the Catawba River. The attack was spearheaded by Lieutenant-Colonel Hall of the Foot Guards who led the Guards' light infantry. It was only when the advanced guard reached the junction of the fords that they were spotted, and a sentry fired his musket to raise the alarm. At that moment the loyalist guides who accompanied Hall fled back to the western bank, leaving the light infantry to their own devices. Hall plunged on straight ahead, across the Wagon Ford branch just as the militia lined their firing positions and started shooting. The Earl Cornwallis followed behind Hall with the rest of his small army, led by the grenadiers of the two Guards battalions. The crossing was far from easy. Sergeant Lamb recorded that the water was breast high, and that "General O'Hara's horse rolled with him down the current nearly 40 yards." Cornwallis managed to coerce the guides to return, and this time he led his force to the right, across Horse Ford. At one point Cornwallis had his horse shot from under him, but he persevered, and soon he gained the far bank, to the right (south) of the main American position. Not only had the main body crossed without serious injury but they were also in a position to roll up the defenders' flank. Meanwhile, Hall's men struggled to the bank where their commander was killed. His men avenged his death by storming the militia positions and the defenders retired up the wooded slopes behind the ford. Davidson was stationed between the two fords, and seeing his two flanks disintegrate, he ordered his men to retire 100 yards. As they fell back Davidson was shot from his saddle by one of the loyalist guides. At that point all resistance ceased as the militia took to their heels, fleeing over the hill into the deep woods behind. The exact death toll is unknown but locals reported that afterwards "the river stunk with dead carcasses."

THE RACE TO THE DAN

Cornwallis brought the rest of his small force across the Catawba River, then sent Tarleton and his British Legion horse to pursue the militia to the east. Tarleton's scouts reported that the local militia were re-forming at Tarrant's Tavern, some six miles from the river. Nearly 300 militia had assembled when Tarleton's men cantered down the road. Inspired by the battle cry "Remember the Cowpens," the riders charged the militia who routed once more, leaving several dead behind them. The two actions had effectively cowed the local militia of Rowan and Mecklenburg counties, both staunchly patriot regions of North Carolina. These militiamen would play no further part in events, and Cornwallis's army was free to move on in pursuit of Morgan and Greene. The new goal for both armies was Trading Ford on the Yadkin River. Conditions for both armies were appalling. One American wrote, "every step being up to our knees in mud, it raining on us all the way."

The American column limped into the small town of Salisbury on the morning of 2 February and Greene sent a message to Brigadier-General Huger. It requested Huger and his Continental Line troops to rendezvous with Morgan's men at Guilford Courthouse if he was more than a day's march from Salisbury when the message reached him. Further to the northeast Morgan was fording the Yadkin River at Trading Ford. Although the river was too deep to wade across, the meticulous Greene had ordered that local rowing boats be gathered at the crossing, and they were used to ferry Morgan's men to the eastern shore. By the early evening his men were across and as they gathered on the far bank in the dusk, Cornwallis's vanguard entered Salisbury. Greene had already departed for Trading Ford, but Cornwallis ordered Colonel O'Hara to try to catch Morgan with his back to the swollen river. O'Hara led the Guards Brigade, the Hessians and Tarleton's British Legion off into the night, pushing hard towards the Yadkin. He reached the river around midnight to find Morgan and Greene safely encamped on the far shore. He had to be content with capturing the American baggage wagons, which could not be transported across the river. The following day Cornwallis arrived and the British and American generals stared at each other across the river for the rest of that day. Late on 4 February the Americans broke camp and resumed their retreat, leaving Cornwallis helpless on the western bank of the Yadkin, waiting for the water level to fall. In the next two days Greene's army marched 47 miles, reaching Guilford Courthouse on the evening of 6 February. The following day

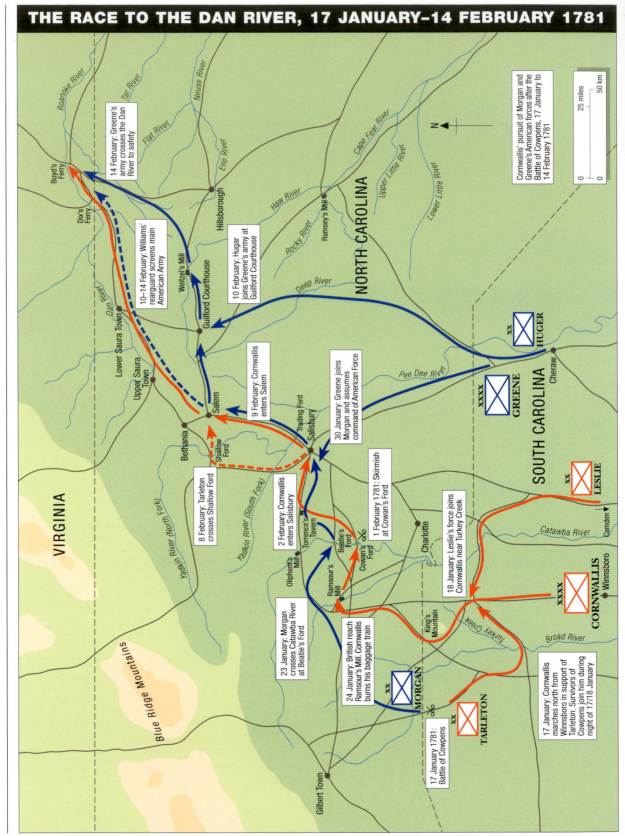

THE RACE TO THE DAN RIVER, 17 JANUARY–14 FEBRUARY 1781

14 February: Greene's army crosses the Dan River to safety

10–14 February: Williams' rearguard screens main American Army

10 February: Hugar joins Greene's army at Guilford Courthouse

Cornwallis' pursuit of Morgan and Greene's American forces after the Battle of Cowpens, 17 January to 14 February 1781

9 February: Cornwallis enters Salem

30 January: Greene joins Morgan and assumes command of American Force

8 February: Tarleton crosses Shallow Ford

2 February: Cornwallis enters Salisbury

1 February 1781: Skirmish at Cowan's Ford

23 January: Morgan crosses Catawba River at Beatie's Ford

24 January: British reach Ramsour's Mill. Cornwallis burns his baggage train

18 January: Leslie's force joins Cornwallis near Turkey Creek

17 January: Cornwallis marches north from Winnsboro in support of Tarleton. Survivors of Cowpens join him during night of 17/18 January

17 January 1781: Battle of Cowpens

VIRGINIA

NORTH CAROLINA

SOUTH CAROLINA

Blue Ridge Mountains

Roanoke River

Tar River

Neuse River

Flat River

Eno River

Haw River

Cape Fear River

Upper Little River

Lower Little River

Dan River

Rocky River

Deep River

Pee Dee River

Yadkin River (North Fork)

Yadkin River (South Fork)

Catawba River

Broad River

Turkey Creek

Boyd's Ferry

Dix's Ferry

Lower Saura Town

Upper Saura Town

Bethania

Hillsborough

Ramsey's Mill

Weitzel's Mill

Guilford Courthouse

Salem

Shallow Ford

Trading Ford

Salisbury

Oliphant's Mill

Torrence's Tavern

Beatie's Ford

Cowan's Ford

Charlotte

Ramsour's Mill

King's Mountain

Cheraw

Camden

Winnsboro

Gilbert Town

HUGAR

GREENE

LESLIE

CORNWALLIS

MORGAN

TARLETON

xx

xxxx

xx

xxxx

xx

xx

N

25 miles

50 km

An American 6-pdr artillery piece being manhandled into position. Greene had four such guns at his disposal during the battle of Guilford Courthouse, commanded by Captain Anthony Singleton of the Continental Artillery.

Brigadier-General Huger arrived with 1,500 reinforcements – four regiments of the Continental Line. Greene considered making a stand near the courthouse, but he decided his army was too small to face Cornwallis's redcoats. He decided to cross the Dan River into Virginia at Boyd's Ferry, and with the river in flood, once again ordered boats to be gathered. Lieutenant-Colonel John Eager Howard's regiment of 280 Delawares and Marylanders would screen the army, supported by the horse and foot of Lee's Legion, and Colonel William Washington's 150 Continental dragoons. Greene planned to give command of the rearguard to Morgan, but by this stage the brigadier was practically incapacitated with sciatica, so command of the new "Light Corps" went to Colonel Otho Williams instead. As Greene wrote: "Great generals are scarce. There are few Morgans to be found around." The temporary incapacitation of the brigadier was a setback for the American cause.

By this time Cornwallis had discovered the presence of Shallows Ford, some ten miles upstream on the Yadkin River. He sent Tarleton and his cavalry to scout the crossing, and finding no opposition, Cornwallis ordered the rest of his army to follow. The army left Salisbury and Trading Ford at dawn on 7 February, and the troops reached the Moravian settlement of Salem two days later. Although neither commander was aware of the fact, the two armies were now only 25 miles apart. On the morning of 10 February Greene led his troops northeast from Guilford Courthouse toward Boyd's Ferry and Irwin's Ferry some 70 miles away. Williams remained behind with his Corps and placed his troops between the two armies, slowly leading Cornwallis away from the main American force. During the next few days Cornwallis, Greene and Williams all moved steadily northeast, with Greene ahead of the rest and further to the east, Williams in the centre and Cornwallis behind furthest west. While intermittent snow showers made conditions unpleasant for the troops, movement at night on roads that were frozen solid proved easier than marching during the day on roads that had turned back to mud. During this period Greene ordered his troops to start marching at 3.00am, stopping only at dusk. Lieutenant-Colonel Lee worked miracles with his cavalry, preventing Tarleton from working his way round on to the road used by Greene's army, but despite Lee's best efforts Tarleton's men succeeded in capturing stragglers from Greene's army during the night of 12/13 February. He informed Cornwallis and by force marching the British moved east, placing them on the same road as Williams' force. Tarleton's men raced ahead but after losing a brief skirmish with Lee's Legion, in which 18 of Tarleton's men were killed, the loyalist troopers hung back. With Greene well on the way to Boyd's Ferry, Williams ordered his men to veer off along the same route; Lee could be relied upon to keep the British at bay. By now all three forces were moving as fast as they possibly could in a race for the river. Williams began to fear the worst and made plans for a last stand to buy more time. However, in the late afternoon of 14 February two messengers from Greene reached Williams, informing him that "all our troops over and the stage is clear … I am ready to receive you and give you a hearty welcome." Colonel O'Hara heard the cheering and realized its import. Greene had safely crossed the Dan at Boyd's Ferry the previous night. Now all the Americans had to do was extricate the Light Corps. Sixteen hours later, at 4.00am on 15 February, Williams' men reached the waiting ferries, and by 9.00am Lee's troopers rode up and were ferried across. Cornwallis's army with Tarleton's dragoons in their van were still some 12 miles behind near Wiley's Farm, south of Irwin's Ferry. Greene had won the "Race to the Dan," and the outmanoeuvred Cornwallis was left on the wrong bank of an impassable barrier.

BETWEEN THE HAW AND THE DAN

Cornwallis faced a dilemma; although he had cleared both North and South Carolina of regular troops, he had failed to destroy Greene's army. His opponent was now out of reach beyond the impassable Dan. He was also far from his supply bases in South Carolina, his army was exhausted and he had lost any method of communication with his superiors in New York and London. He was on his own. He considered trying to find a way across the river using rafts, but Greene's men would be able to counter any attempt and cut the attackers to pieces. Cornwallis decided to retire to Hillsborough, which was known to be a predominantly loyalist region. There his troops could recover from their ordeal and fresh provisions could be gathered. Once in Hillsborough, Cornwallis issued a proclamation calling on all loyalists to rise up and join him in defeating the rebels.

Greene's army, encamped around Halifax Courthouse a few miles north of the Dan River, was also in a poor condition, but at least he was close to his supply bases in Virginia. He could also count on reinforcements from the Virginia militia. To maintain pressure on the British, on 18 February he sent his Light Corps back across the river into North Carolina. Lee's Legion and Brigadier-General Andrew Picken's militia brigade were ordered to harry the British, and to try to prevent them from recruiting local loyalists into their army. "Light Horse Harry" Lee met with almost immediate success. He learned that a force of 400 local loyalist militia commanded by Colonel John Pyle was marching east along the Haw River to join Cornwallis's army and on 25 February Lee rode to intercept them. As the cavalry approached, Pyle and his men mistook Lee's green-coated dragoons for Tarleton's men, and by the time they realized their mistake the cavalry were among them, riding down the militia in an engagement that became known as "Pyle's massacre." Only a handful of loyalists survived and the skirmish put paid to any further active loyalist support for Cornwallis.

Meanwhile, Greene brought the rest of his army across the river, but kept the bulk of his force beyond the reach of Cornwallis. The British commander duly moved his camp to the junction of the Haw River and Stinking Quarter Creek, to be better placed to march on Greene's force if the opportunity arose. He was desperate for a decisive engagement – his men were short of food and under the constant attrition of skirmishes and disease his army was dwindling as fast as that of his opponent was growing.

A wounded American officer tries to direct his men. General Edward Stevens commanding the American second defensive line was wounded in the thigh during the battle, but with his help his Virginia militia performed well, their fire exacting a heavy toll on the advancing British regulars.

WEITZEL'S MILL

On 6 March Cornwallis was presented with an opportunity to destroy part of Greene's army. His patrols reported that the Americans "were posted carelessly at separate plantations for the convenience of subsisting." Greene's main army was encamped several miles north of Reedy Fork Creek, while other units were posted further to the east and south. The majority of the Light Corps commanded by Colonel Williams was posted on the south side of Reedy Fork Creek, in several locations along the road that connected Hillsborough and Guilford Courthouse. Cornwallis decided to attack Williams' force, hoping to isolate it and destroy it in detail. Using the cover of early morning mist, he planned to advance Tarleton's men up the road to drive a wedge between the commands of Williams and Campbell, then to pin them while Webster's men destroyed each American formation in turn.

Tarleton's dragoons overran the militia outpost on the Alamance Creek, then thundered north up the road to Weitzel's Mill. Two miles further on he ran into the pickets guarding Campbell's encampment, but the prompt arrival of Lee's Legion and Washington's cavalry prevented the British Legion from launching a charge. Protected by the cavalry, Campbell fell back to Weitzel's Mill with the British following close behind them. Tarleton ignored American stragglers and intermittent harassing fire from isolated pockets of American militiamen in the woods beside the road. Instead he pushed the Americans back for another eight miles until they reached Reedy Fork Creek. Williams' Light Corps also broke camp and marched north, taking up covering positions on the north bank of the creek, where they could cover the three fords in the area.

By mid-afternoon Williams and Campbell met by the river, and devised a plan to extricate Campbell's brigade without it being caught as it forded the river. A rearguard was needed, and Williams selected Colonel William Preston's Virginia Rifle battalion to cover the retreat, supported by the rifles of Colonel Crocket's men – a total of 360 men in all. Howard's Continental regulars were stationed to the right of the main ford supported by the bulk of Campbell's militia, while Lee's Legion formed up on their left, covering the smaller Horse Ford. As

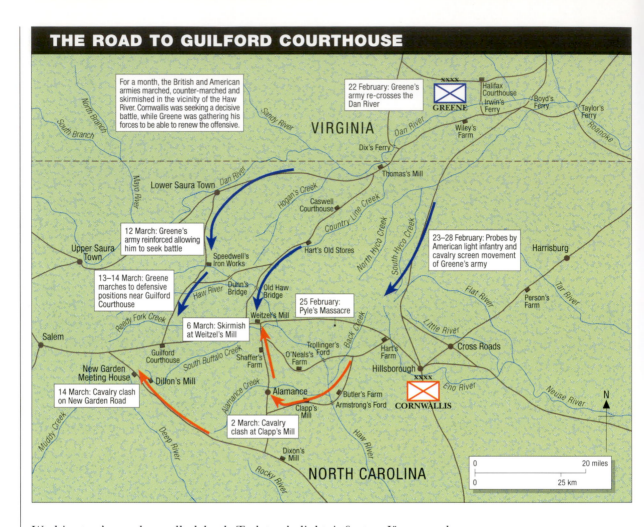

For a month, the British and American armies marched, counter-marched and skirmished in the vicinity of the Haw River. Cornwallis was seeking a decisive battle, while Greene was gathering his forces to be able to renew the offensive.

22 February: Greene's army re-crosses the Dan River

12 March: Greene's army reinforced allowing him to seek battle

23–28 February: Probes by American light infantry and cavalry screen movement of Greene's army

13–14 March: Greene marches to defensive positions near Guilford Courthouse

25 February: Pyle's Massacre

6 March: Skirmish at Weitzel's Mill

14 March: Cavalry clash on New Garden Road

2 March: Cavalry clash at Clapp's Mill

VIRGINIA

NORTH CAROLINA

Washington's cavalry pulled back Tarleton's light infantry, Jägers and cavalry attacked Preston's riflemen, who were stationed on the high wooded ground to the south of the fords. Cornwallis arrived and, when it became clear that the riflemen were reluctant to flee, ordered the 33rd Foot into the attack, followed by the 23rd Fusiliers and the 71st Highlanders. Faced with an attack by overwhelming numbers, Preston's riflemen broke and ran back to the fords. The 23rd and 71st followed Preston's men towards Horse Ford, while the rest of the army surged on towards the main ford itself. As Lee rallied Preston's men, the British regulars formed up for an attack across both fords. To support the assault Cornwallis brought up his four artillery pieces, and deployed them on the high ground immediately east of the mill, where they could sweep the far bank of either ford. Meanwhile, the light infantrymen of the Foot Guards had discovered that the third ford (known as the Western Ford) was unguarded and they crossed then moved north, following the curve of the river that led to the north bank of the main ford.

Lieutenant-Colonel Webster had already tried to lead the 33rd Foot across the main ford on the heels of Preston's fleeing riflemen, but the heavy fire of Howard's infantry drove them back. While the Jägers provided covering fire, Webster reorganized his troops and prepared

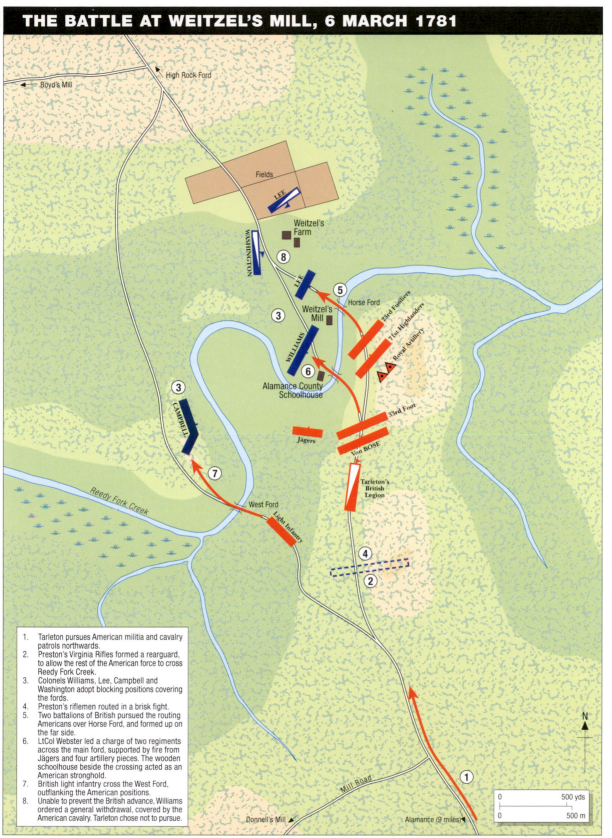

THE BATTLE AT WEITZEL'S MILL, 6 MARCH 1781

Boyd's Mill

High Rock Ford

Fields

LEE

Weitzel's Farm

WASHINGTON

8

LEE

WILLIAMS

5

Horse Ford

23rd Fusiliers

71st Highlanders

Royal Artillery

3

Weitzel's Mill

6

Alamance County Schoolhouse

3

CAMPBELL

Jägers

33rd Foot

Von BOSE

7

West Ford

Light Infantry

Tarleton's British Legion

Reedy Fork Creek

4

2

1. Tarleton pursues American militia and cavalry patrols northwards.
2. Preston's Virginia Rifles formed a rearguard, to allow the rest of the American force to cross Reedy Fork Creek.
3. Colonels Williams, Lee, Campbell and Washington adopt blocking positions covering the fords.
4. Preston's riflemen routed in a brisk fight.
5. Two battalions of British pursued the routing Americans over Horse Ford, and formed up on the far side.
6. LtCol Webster led a charge of two regiments across the main ford, supported by fire from Jägers and four artillery pieces. The wooden schoolhouse beside the crossing acted as an American stronghold.
7. British light infantry cross the West Ford, outflanking the American positions.
8. Unable to prevent the British advance, Williams ordered a general withdrawal, covered by the American cavalry. Tarleton chose not to pursue.

Mill Road

Donnell's Mill

1

Alamance (9 miles)

N

0 500 yds
0 500 m

them for a more deliberate assault across the creek. On the far bank,
Williams was well aware of what was coming and, as the 23rd and
71st were already probing across Horse Ford, it appeared his line was in
danger of being outflanked. His fears were heightened when the British
light infantry appeared on his right flank. Williams ordered Howard and
Campbell to begin withdrawing their men, while Lee's Legion were
to cover the retreat. Unfortunately for Lee the British were already
crossing Horse Ford, and most of his cavalry were pinned. Lee still had
his 90-man infantry detachment, split between a small log-built
schoolhouse that covered the ford and a small knoll just to the north of
the crossing point. He later recounted how mist and musket smoke
clung to the creek, and out of it he saw a British column appear,
splashing across the ford with a mounted officer at its head. It was
Webster leading the 33rd Foot in a second attack. Lee's infantry opened
fire, but somehow Webster survived and the column kept coming. As the
British approached the north bank, Lee gave orders for his men to
retire, and as the American foot withdrew Lee and Washington's cavalry
covered the retreat.

Cornwallis ordered his Hessians to join in the pursuit and unleashed
Tarleton's dragoons, who cantered up the road towards the north. They
were brought to a halt by the line of American cavalry supported by
Lee's foot, and Tarleton declined to charge allowing the Americans
to withdraw. Tarleton followed for two more miles, while the rest of
Cornwallis's army camped for the night on the north bank of Reedy
Fork Creek. It has been estimated that both sides lost 30–40 men in the
skirmish, mainly from the 33rd Foot and Preston's Virginia Rifles.
Cornwallis had failed to destroy a major part of Greene's army and, as

Williams led his men north, he must have been more than content with the performance of his men. Cornwallis declined to pursue and by so doing he lost any advantage he had gained. Greene's army was about to be reinforced and the British advantage in numbers and quality of men would never be so marked. The next time the two armies met, the odds would be stacked more heavily in the American favor.

The following day Cornwallis moved his men further west into the southwest corner of Guilford County, where he set up camp near the Quaker community surrounding Deep River Friends Meeting House. Although Greene was still not ready to take on Cornwallis's army, he planned to take the offensive as soon as his reinforcements arrived. He could then give Cornwallis the full-scale battle the British commander had been seeking. Both sides were well aware that the outcome of the forthcoming engagement could well decide the fate of the Carolinas, if not the outcome of the war.

FORCES ENGAGED AT WEITZEL'S MILL, 6 MARCH 1781

BRITISH
Lieutenant-General Charles, Earl Cornwallis (Commander-in-Chief)
Von Bose Regiment (Hessians) (in reserve) – 313 men
Royal Artillery detachment; 4 x 3-pdr "grasshopper" guns – 73 men

Lieutenant-Colonel Banastre Tarleton's Command
British Legion (cavalry) – 174 men
Jaeger Detachment (Hessians) – 94 men
Light Infantry Companies, Foot Guards – 80 men

Lieutenant-Colonel Webster's Command
23rd Fusiliers – 258 men
33rd Foot – 322 men
2nd Bn., 71st Highlanders – 212 men

AMERICANS
Colonel Otho Williams' Command, "The Light Corps"
Lieutenant-Colonel Howard, Delaware and Maryland Continental Light Infantry – 226 men
Major Rowland's Virginia Rifle Corps – 114 men
Colonel Crocket's Virginia Rifle Battalion – 232 men
Lieutenant-Colonel Harrison's North Carolina Militia – 50 men
Colonel William Washington, 1st/3rd Continental Light Dragoons – 100 men

Colonel William Campbell's Command ("Pickens' Brigade")
Colonel Campbell's Virginia Rifle Corps – 54 men
Colonel Preston's Virginia Rifle Battalion – 124 men
Lieutenant-Colonel Williams' North Carolina Militia – 36 men
Colonel Moore's North Carolina Militia – 45 men
Colonel McCall's Militia Cavalry – 120 men
Lee's Legion (cavalry) – 90 men
       (infantry) – 90 men

THE BATTLE OF GUILFORD COURTHOUSE

THE SKIRMISH ON THE NEW GARDEN ROAD

On 10 March General Greene wrote to Thomas Jefferson to say: "the Militia have indeed flocked in from various quarters." Over 1,000 militiamen from North Carolina had entered the American camp led by Brigadier-Generals John Butler and Thomas Eaton. Brigadier-General Robert Lawson had also brought in about 700 Virginia militia, to augment the militiamen already serving under Brigadier-General Edward Stevens. Even more importantly, "Baron" von Steuben had been recruiting Virginians into the Continental Army, and around 400 of these recruits had arrived and were added to the ranks of the two regular Virginia regiments. The veteran Maryland and Delaware regulars of Howard's Continental Light Infantry battalion had been split between the two Maryland regiments, and Howard was appointed as second-in-command of the 1st Maryland Regiment. On 14 March Greene marched his men south from their encampment near Speedwell's Ironworks towards Guilford Courthouse, where he planned to offer battle on ground of his own choosing. The die was about to be cast, and morale in the army was high. All told, Greene commanded around 4,400 men, including 1,600 regulars, and most considered this

In this winter scene of a regiment of infantry on the march the engraver has captured the miserable conditions faced by 18th-century troops during a winter campaign. Both Cornwallis and Greene suffered steady attrition of their armies through sickness and injury resulting from campaigning in such harsh conditions.

Militiamen felling trees to create a temporary defensive position. Greene ensured that his marching camps were fortified, and that, where time permitted, his troops enjoyed the benefits of static positions. During the night following his defeat at Guilford Courthouse his men prepared defences against a British attack that never came.

more than enough to take on Cornwallis's 2,200 British regulars. Two days later Cornwallis's scouts informed him that the Americans were on the move and had reached Guilford Courthouse. That evening the reports were confirmed and Cornwallis issued the orders for his army to march against that of his American opponent. Greene's army spent the night encamped around Guilford Courthouse. The two armies were now only 12 miles apart.

The American commander spent a sleepless night, worried that the threatened rain might soak his army's powder, or that Cornwallis would launch a surprise night-attack up the New Garden Road. He was right to be concerned; Cornwallis was indeed considering an immediate attack in the darkness where his better-trained regulars would be at an advantage. Greene directed "Light Horse Harry" Lee to take his Legion of approximately 160 horse and foot, and 100 of Colonel William Campbell's riflemen west up the New Garden Road to form an advanced screen, three miles from the main army. Lee then ordered Lieutenant James Heard and his troop to "place himself near the British camp, and to report from time to time such occurrences as might happen." Heard ranged as far as the British outposts around Deep River Friends Meeting House, and at 2.00am he reported that the redcoats were stirring. On Lee's orders he hid his men in the woods beside the New Garden Meeting House, halfway between the two armies. At 4.00am he reported that he heard the rumbling of wagon wheels, and Tarleton's cavalry patrols were sighted patrolling along the road. He added that he was sure a "general movement" was underway; a report that was passed on to General Greene. In fact what he heard was the passage of Cornwallis's few remaining ambulance and baggage wagons, escorted by a small detachment of British Legion infantry and local loyalist militia. The baggage train would take no part in the ensuing battle, and turned off the road at the Meeting House, heading on a southern fork towards Bell's Mill. Cornwallis had roused his army around 3.00am and had sent his baggage off under escort, followed an hour later by his advanced guard, commanded by Tarleton. The cavalry commander had 270 men under his command – his own British Legion cavalry, 100 light infantrymen from the Foot Guards and 84 Hessian Jägers. Cornwallis followed behind with the bulk of the army. By 5.00am Tarleton was approaching the New Friends Meeting House junction when suddenly his men were fired on from the woods. Heard and his men had opened fire to warn Lee of the danger, then his men mounted their horses and rode off up the New Garden Road.

At around 4.30am Lee was ordered to take the whole Legion down the road to make contact with the British. Lee obliged and, leaving the infantry to follow on behind, he cantered ahead with his cavalry. As the column was approaching New Ground Meeting House they met Heard's patrol. Lee was four miles west of Greene's army so he elected to fall back towards his infantry, then make a stand. Tarleton's men gave chase but Lee's rearguard, commanded by a Captain Armstrong, held the loyalist cavalry at a distance with carbine fire. The rest of Lee's men turned around in a section of the road that was described as a "long lane with high curved fences on either side." Armstrong's men fell back and as Tarleton advanced he found his men were restricted in the lane. Lee's Legion charged, and "Tarleton retired with celerity." Lee's men pursued the loyalist cavalry as far as the Quaker meeting house, only to meet Cornwallis's infantry coming the other way. It was the turn of Lee's cavalry to retire, but once they reached their supporting infantry they rallied, and the skirmish continued for another 30 minutes before Lee retired towards Greene's army. Lee reached the American lines shortly after noon, and his men were ordered to take position to the left of the first American line.

GREENE'S DISPOSITIONS

General Greene had studied the area surrounding Guilford Courthouse during the "Race to the Dan" six weeks before, and he was well aware of the defensive possibilities of the location. To many the terrain was unremarkable. In Colonel Lee's words:

"Guilford Courthouse, erected near the great State road, is situated on the brow of a declivity, which ascends gradually with an undulating slope for about half a mile. It terminates in a small vale, intersected by a rivulet. On the right of the road is open ground with some few copse of wood until you gain the step of the descent, where you see thick glades of brushy wood reaching across the rivulet; on the left of the road from the court-house a deep forest of lofty trees, which terminates nearly in a line with the termination of a field on the opposite side of the road. Below the forest is a small piece of open ground, which appeared to have been cultivated in corn the preceding summer. This small field was long, reaching close to the swamp bordering upon the rivulet."

Greene realized something Lee had missed – the battlefield was divided into three distinct areas. The first contained a series of open fields, behind which was a fence, giving militia a clear field of fire, a modicum of cover and an avenue of retreat into the woods behind them. The woods themselves provided cover for a second line, and would disorganize any troops advancing through them in close order. Once an attacker had reached the edge of these trees, and had avoided being disrupted by the small ravine, they would find themselves at the edge of the small open clearing, facing the slight rise on which sat the courthouse. While each successive line was a less than ideal defensive position, the three taken together created a succession of defensible positions that could be used to wear down an attacker before they reached the third and final line.

Greene had also taken heed of the advice and example of Brigadier-General Morgan, concerning the commanding of militia. "If they fight, you will beat Cornwallis; if not, he will beat you and perhaps cut your regulars to pieces … put the militia in the centre, with some picked troops in their rear, with orders to shoot down the first man that runs." Although Greene was less draconian, he understood how to get the most from these fragile troops, and made his dispositions accordingly. He also used the example of Morgan's deployment at Cowpens, which was ideally suited to the staged defence Greene had planned for the forthcoming battle.

Greene deployed his army during the morning of 15 March, and once in position, his men waited for the British to arrive. He deployed in three successive lines. In the first were his least reliable men, the 1,000 men of the North Carolina militia, divided into two brigades. To the right of the road were the 500 men of Brigadier-General Thomas Eaton's brigade – men from Halifax and Warren counties in the northern part of the colony. Their left flank was anchored on the new Garden Road. To their left, lining a rail fence was Brigadier-General John Butler's brigade of 500 men raised in Orange and Granville county, as well as in Guilford county itself. Apart from the Granville men these were local militia. In front of these militiamen to the west was a series of small open fields, full of mud and stubble. Greene anchored his flanks with more reliable units. On the right of Eaton's brigade were 200 riflemen from Colonel Charles Lynch's Virginia battalion, plus a detachment of up to 110 veterans, regular light infantry from Delaware, commanded by Captain Robert Kirkwood. These light troops were supported by Lieutenant-Colonel William Washington's cavalry, 86 dragoons from the 1st and 3rd Continental Light Dragoons, both Virginia regiments. Kirkwood's and Washington's men were veterans of Cowpens, and knew how the battle should be fought: retiring to secondary positions, re-forming and fighting again. During the morning when the advanced guard commanded by Lee returned down the New Garden Road, they were allocated a position on the extreme left of the American line, beyond the left flank of Butler's brigade. "Light Horse Harry" Lee took charge of the flank, commanding the 82 infantry and 75 cavalry of his own Legion as well as Colonel William Campbell's 200 rifle-armed Virginian mountain men, some of whom were veterans of King's Mountain. Right in the centre of this first defensive line was the artillery, two 6-pdr guns commanded by Captain Anthony Singleton. They were positioned so they had a clear field of fire down the road to the west. Lee approved of

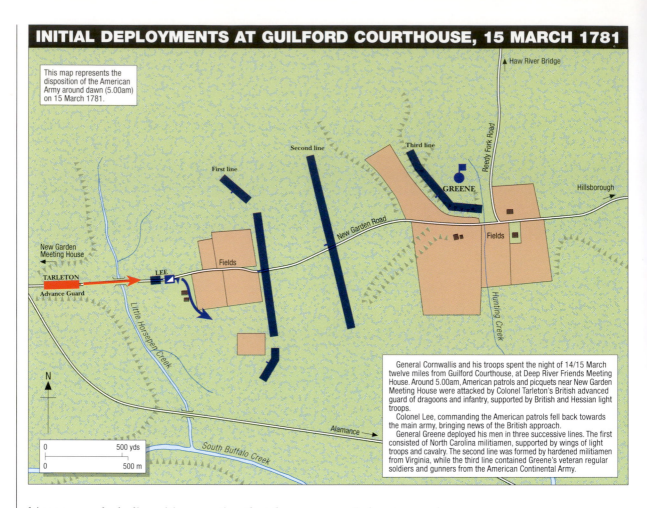

This map represents the disposition of the American Army around dawn (5.00am) on 15 March 1781.

Haw River Bridge

Second line

Third line

First line

Reedy Fork Road

GREENE

Hillsborough

New Garden Road

Fields

New Garden Meeting House

Fields

TARLETON

Advance Guard

LEE

Little Horsepen Creek

Hunting Creek

N

Alamance

South Buffalo Creek

| 0 | 500 yds |
| 0 | 500 m |

General Cornwallis and his troops spent the night of 14/15 March twelve miles from Guilford Courthouse, at Deep River Friends Meeting House. Around 5.00am, American patrols and picquets near New Garden Meeting House were attacked by Colonel Tarleton's British advanced guard of dragoons and infantry, supported by British and Hessian light troops.
   Colonel Lee, commanding the American patrols fell back towards the main army, bringing news of the British approach.
   General Greene deployed his men in three successive lines. The first consisted of North Carolina militiamen, supported by wings of light troops and cavalry. The second line was formed by hardened militiamen from Virginia, while the third line contained Greene's veteran regular soldiers and gunners from the American Continental Army.

his commander's dispositions, noting that the men were "advantageously posted."

Approximately 300 yards to the rear (east) of the first line was a second line, this time consisting of Virginia militia. As these men had experienced commanders and contained a significant proportion of former Continental Army soldiers whose enlistment had expired, Greene expected them to be more reliable than the Carolinians in front of them. Greene knew well that where militia were concerned, reliability was a relative term. To the north of the road, and directly to the rear of Eaton's brigade, were the 600 men of Brigadier-General Robert Lawson's brigade. To their left were a similar number of militia, forming the brigade of Brigadier-General Edward Stevens. At Camden these Virginia militia had fled the field without firing a single shot and, to expunge this shame, their commander was determined that his men would acquit themselves with honour. If Greene was unwilling to heed Morgan's advice concerning militia, Stevens was taking no chances. Twenty yards behind his line he stationed a string of riflemen, with orders to "shoot the first man who might run." The flanks of these two brigades were unprotected, but Greene's plan was that at the right moment the experienced commanders of the flank troops of the first line would retire their men, re-forming on the flanks of the second line. As for the Carolinian militia, they were expected to retire after firing a

American infantrymen of a Continental Line regiment around a campfire. Despite Greene's abilities, his army was frequently short of food. Conditions for the British were even worse.

few shots, and the Virginians were ready for the militia in front of them to pass through their ranks. Clearly this was a risky manoeuvre, as there was a significant chance the second line would be swept away too. Greene's dispositions were nothing if not daring, and were influenced as much by rudimentary psychology as they were by tactics.

Five hundred yards to the rear of the second line, and at the eastern edge of the small clearing stood the third and final defensive line, the 1,400 regular infantrymen of the Continental Line. The left of the line was held by Colonel Benjamin Ford's 2nd Maryland Regiment, and they faced to the southwest, refusing the left flank of Greene's position. On their right and facing directly west was the 1st Maryland Regiment, under the command of Colonel John Gunby. The experienced Lieutenant-Colonel John Eager Howard acted as his second-in-command. These two regiments formed Colonel Otho Williams' brigade. Both formations contained approximately 360 men. Immediately to the right of Gunby's battalion were Greene's remaining two guns, both 6-pdrs, under the command of Lieutenant Ebenezer Finley. Greene's plan was that when the first line retired, the two guns commanded by Singleton would be rushed down the road and would deploy alongside Finley's guns. To the right of the guns and following the line of the slope were the two regiments of Brigadier-General Isaac Huger's brigade. The left-hand regiment was Lieutenant-Colonel Samuel Hawes' 5th Virginia Regiment, while the right flank of Greene's line was anchored by the 4th Virginia

Regiment, commanded by Colonel John Green. Each regiment consisted of just under 400 men. Of these four regiments, the 1st Maryland was an experienced, battle-hardened formation, while the 2nd Maryland was a new and untested formation, consisting of fresh recruits and a leavening of survivors from other Maryland regiments that took part in the Camden campaign. Both Virginia regiments were reliable, reasonably experienced and well led. In front of this third line, the ground sloped down into what has been described as a small natural amphitheatre, a depression formed by the converging slopes of three low ridges. This area had been cleared by local farmers, creating a patch of fallow ground approximately 1,000 yards long, north–south, and 250 yards wide. Further behind the American positions and to the south of Guilford Courthouse was another area of fields, bounded by unkempt hedgerows. Behind the American line the forest began again, hiding the two roads that ran north and east from the clearing. That morning, Green had sent his baggage wagons along the northern road towards the Speedwell Ironworks, some 18 miles to the northeast. It was a sensible precaution.

Once his dispositions had been made, Greene toured the units, taking particular care to encourage the North Carolina militia. After reminding them that they fought for their homes and families as well as for liberty, he told them what he expected of them – to fire two volleys at the British advancing towards them, then to fall back. He was using Morgan's method of setting reasonable limits to what was expected of his militia. He repeated the orders to the Virginians in the second line, adding that they were required to open their ranks to let the Carolinians through before firing their volleys. The regular units and riflemen on the flanks of the first line were ordered to fall back when the militia did, then re-form on the flanks of each subsequent line. As for the regulars in the third line, they needed no special orders. They were expected to stand and fight. Greene had done everything he could, and he returned to his position in the centre of the third line. What happened next would depend on the actions of Cornwallis.

CORNWALLIS'S DEPLOYMENT

At noon the American first line caught sight of the advanced guard of the British column as it approached Little Horsepen Creek, some 800 yards west of the waiting militia. As the first British troops forded the stream, Captain Singleton opened the battle by firing his two 6-pdr guns, with little effect. Cornwallis was in the van of his army, so he halted his men, and ordered up his three 3-pdr "galloper" guns, commanded by Lieutenant MacLeod of the Royal Artillery. While the guns fought their own private duel, Cornwallis deployed his army. He was unsure what lay ahead, even though he had passed down the road six weeks before. Seeing that the woods were relatively dense on the left of the road, and the right appeared more open, he resolved to place the main weight of his attack against the enemy's left flank.

The 212 men of the 2nd Battalion of the veteran 71st Highlanders were deployed in a two-deep line to the right of the road, immediately behind a small farm known as the Hoskins House. The battalion was commanded by Lieutenant-Colonel Duncan McPherson. To the right of the blue-bonneted Scots were the 313 Hessians of Lieutenant-Colonel Johann Christian DuBuy's von Bose Regiment. Major-General Alexander Leslie commanded the two formations. In reserve, behind his main line, Leslie could call on the assistance of the 200 men of 1st Battalion, Foot Guards, commanded by Lieutenant-Colonel Norton. Technically, the formation formed part of the Guards Brigade, commanded by Colonel Charles O'Hara, but it appears that battlefield control of the Guards battalion was ceded to Leslie before the firing began. On the left, or north, side of the road, Cornwallis deployed the two regiments of Lieutenant-Colonel James Webster's brigade. First came the 23rd Fusiliers, also known as the "Royal Welsh Fusiliers." The regiment consisted of 258 men, and was commanded by Lieutenant-Colonel Nesbitt Balfour. On their left were the 33rd Foot, commanded by Webster himself. The formation contained 322 men. In support of Webster's brigade and on their left flank were the detachment of 84 Jägers, and the two light-infantry companies of the Guards (approximately 100 men in total). As a reserve, O'Hara's command consisted of the 2nd Battalion, Foot Guards, and the two combined companies of Guard Grenadiers. Together, the two units contained about 420 men. Behind O'Hara, and deployed in column on the road, were the 174 dragoons of Lieutenant-Colonel Banastre Tarleton's British Legion. Cornwallis was keeping these loyalist cavalrymen in reserve, ready to be unleashed in pursuit of a broken enemy.

His dispositions made, Cornwallis gave the signal to attack. The artillery ceased firing, the battle proper was about to begin.

ORDER OF BATTLE
GUILFORD COURTHOUSE, 15 MARCH 1781

BRITISH

Commanding officer: Lieutenant-General Charles, Lord Cornwallis

Lieutenant-Colonel Webster's Brigade
23rd Foot (Fusiliers) – 258 men
33rd Foot – 322 men

Major-General Leslie's Brigade
2nd Battalion, 71st Foot (Highlanders), – 212 men
Von Bose Regiment (Hessians) – 313 men

Colonel O'Hara's Guards Brigade
1st Battalion, Foot Guards – 300 men
2nd Battalion, Foot Guards – 300 men
Grenadier Detachment (drawn from Foot Guards) – 120 men

Reserves (directly controlled by Cornwallis)
Colonel Tarleton's British Legion (Dragoons and Foot) – 174 men
Jägers (Hessians) – 97 men
Light Infantry Detachment (drawn from Foot Guards) – 120 men
Royal Artillery (Captain MacLeod), 3 x 3-pdrs

Baggage Escort (not present at battle)
Detachment, British Legion (Dragoons) – 20 men
North Carolina Loyalist Volunteers – 130 men

AMERICANS
Commanding officer: Major-General Nathaniel Greene

First Line
Brigadier-General Butler's North Carolina Militia Brigade – 500 men
Brigadier-General Eaton's North Carolina Militia Brigade – 500 men
Campbell's Virginia Rifles – 200 men
Lee's Legion (Dragoons) – 75 men
Lee's Legion (Infantry) – 82 men
Lynch's Virginia Rifles – 200 men
Colonel Washington's 1st/3rd Continental Dragoons – 86 men
1st Continental Artillery Detachment, 2 x 6-pdrs

Second Line
Brigadier-General Lawson's Virginia Militia Brigade – 600 men
Brigadier-General Steven's Virginia Militia Brigade – 600 men

Third Line
Brigadier-General Huger's Brigade:
4th Virginia Regiment – 400 men
5th Virginia Regiment – 400 men

Colonel Williams' Brigade
1st Maryland Regiment – 360 men
2nd Maryland Regiment – 360 men

1st Continental Artillery Detachment, 2 x 6-pdrs

THE FIRST LINE – "BAYONETS FIXED AND MUSKETS SLOPED"

The North Carolina militiamen lining the split-rail fence waiting for the British to attack must have been extremely nervous. Many had never seen action before, and although Greene had told them he only expected them to fire two volleys before running, many doubted if they could face the professional and battle-hardened soldiers who were deploying in front of them. Major Richard Harrison of Granville County was in Butler's brigade, on the left (southern) side of the New Garden Road. While he was waiting, he penned a note to his wife and newborn daughter: "It is scarcely possible to paint the agitations of my mind, struggling with two of the greatest events that are in nature at one time." To ease the men, "Light Horse Harry" Lee rode up the line of Butler's men as well as his own, calling out that he "had whipped them three times that morning, and could do it again." Shortly after noon, when Captain Singleton's 6-pdr guns opened fire, the British came into view, halted for a bit, then deployed into line on either side of the road. At first, the British line was shorter than that of the Americans, whose flanks curved inwards slightly, to provide some degree of enfilading fire. Then, as the artillery duel played itself out shortly before 1.00pm, Cornwallis sent his reserves up into the front line; the German Jägers and the light infantry companies of the Foot Guards on his left and the 1st Battalion, Foot Guards, on the right. The British line was now approximately the same length as the one it was about to attack.

Cornwallis had no clear idea of what to expect, but he realized that the troops in front of him represented less than a quarter of the American army, and were militia, not regulars. He correctly surmised that Greene had copied Morgan's deployment from Cowpens, and had arrayed his army in more than one line, probably saving his regulars for the last stage of the battle. Cornwallis knew how to deal with militia, as he had watched them run from the field at Camden when threatened with the bayonet. He would advance his line, then rearrange his formation to repeat the process with any subsequent lines of defence his men met in the woods.

The exact time the British started their advance is unclear, but most accounts agree it was around 1.00pm. Two regiments advanced in line on each side of the New Garden Road, creating a line some 1,000 yards long. It was a martial spectacle, and witnesses record the British advance, with muskets at the shoulder, and bayonets fixed, drums and colors to the fore. For the waiting North Carolina militia, it must have been terrifying. Brushing aside the split-rail fencing at the western end of the small enclosures, the British and Hessians advanced through the muddy corn stubble and up the slight rise looking "steady and guarded, but firm and [with] determined resolution." The attackers had to advance across approximately 400 yards of open, muddy ground before they reached the fence at the eastern end of the open fields. Behind the fence the American militia waited, and as Sergeant Lamb of the 23rd Fusiliers recalled, at 200 yards, as the attackers crossed another fence, the enemy "had their arms presented, and resting on the rail fence … They were taking aim with the nicest precision." To avoid any faltering, Colonel Webster rode forward in front of the 23rd crying, "Come on, my brave Fusiliers!" The advance then continued in perfect silence, save the beat of the drummers. Sixty yards further on, with the British line about 140 yards from the fence, the militia fired.

To the south of the road, Captain Dugald Stuart of the 71st Highlanders recalled the effectiveness of the militiamen's initial volley: "one half of the Highlanders dropped on that spot." Once the white smoke cleared, William Montgomery of Butler's Brigade claimed the British fallen looked like "the scattering stalks in a wheatfield, when the harvest man has passed over it with his cradle." Effective though the militia volley was, it wasn't enough to deter the British redcoats. Encouraged by their officers and sergeants, the three British and one Hessian regiment dressed their ranks (men from the rear rank moving forward to plug the gaps), and the advance continued over the bodies of the dead and wounded. The attack was pressed home "in profound silence, with bayonets fixed and muskets sloped." Once they reached point-blank range, some 50 yards from the split-rail fence, all four regiments halted, presented their muskets, and fired a single, devastating volley. Great gaps were blown in the American line. A local

A local blacksmith and his assistant repairing and forging weapons. Greene made full use of local suppliers to provision and equip his army during the Guilford Courthouse Campaign. While arms came from Virginia, clothing and shoes were provided by tradesmen in the townships of northern North Carolina.

officer, Captain Arthur Forbis, who commanded a company of 25 men on the American left, was hit twice, in the neck and the leg. As he lay mortally wounded he called on his men to stand and fight. Few listened. As the British followed up their volley with a steady advance, the majority of the militia turned and fled. Greene had asked for two or three volleys, and he got one. The British Commissary officer Charles Stedman wrote afterwards that, "the enemy did not wait the shock, but retreated behind the second line." Not all the militia ran, and some like the wounded Forbis remained at the fence. On the flanks, the regulars and Continentals wheeled so they could enfilade the flanking British regiments – the 33rd Foot to the north and the von Bose Regiment to the south. To counter this new threat, Cornwallis threw in his reserves, Norton's 1st Battalion, Foot Guards, being ordered to support the Hessians on the right of the line, and the Jägers and Guard light infantry companies doing the same on the British left flank. The fire of Captain Kirkwood's Delaware company and Lynch's Virginia Rifles also forced Webster to react, swinging his 33rd Foot slightly to the left to prevent his line being enfiladed as it passed. The 23rd Fusiliers also veered slightly to the left as they charged Eaton's militia brigade to their front, as the militia line overlapped the advancing British regiment. To avoid creating a gap in the British centre near the road, Cornwallis ordered O'Hara to advance with the 2nd Battalion, Foot Guards, and the Guard Grenadier companies, to plug the hole. When the militia ran, Lee tried to rally the men of Butler's brigade, but apart from a few militiamen, most just threw away their arms and ran. Lee even threatened to ride the routers down with his cavalry, but the threat went unheeded. Although critical of the North Carolina militia as a whole, Lee spoke approvingly of the Carolinians who attached themselves to Campbell's riflemen, and fought on after their companions fled. As the militia along the fence routed, the two flanks of the American first line were in danger of being isolated. Lynch and Kirkwood gave the orders to fall back to the positions allocated to them on the extreme right flank of the second line, their retreat covered by Washington's cavalry. Pausing briefly to engage the British, these infantrymen on the flank then continued their orderly retirement to take up a fresh position on the right flank of the American third line. Washington's cavalrymen retired back to the south of Greene's final line, re-forming, some 300 yards south of the 2nd Maryland Regiment.

The situation was far more confused on the American left flank. Under pressure from the Hessians and then 1st Battalion, Foot Guards, Lee's Legion and Campbell's Rifles fell back. Lee retired southeast, and rather than forming up on the left flank of the second line, he headed further south into the dense woods, drawing the Hessians and Guardsmen behind him. In effect this became a separate fight, a private battle fought around a slight hillock in deep woods, some 1,300 yards south of the New Garden Road. In the process both sides lost the use of a portion of their army. For the British, this meant almost 25 per cent of their total force. At a time when the hard-pressed attackers needed every soldier they had, this would have a profound influence on the course of the battle. From that point on, the already outnumbered British were courting with disaster, as they had barely enough men left to fight. Cornwallis had committed all of his reserves, save the dragoons of the British Legion, and the main battle had yet to be fought.

THE SECOND LINE – "AN ACTION OF ALMOST INFINITE DIVERSITY"

As the British pursued the militia into the woods they found themselves in an unfamiliar environment, and their formations became disordered. The lines broke up into small groups who threaded a path through the trees and undergrowth. The regulars were trained to fight in dense formations, relying on the combined firepower of musketry or the close cohesion of a massed bayonet charge to win the day. In this alien environment these small groups of isolated redcoats were engulfed by the forest, and many lost contact with the rest of their formations. 500 yards into the woods lay the second American line, the Virginia militiamen of Lawson's brigade to the north of the road, and those of General Stevens to the south. In addition, the regulars and riflemen who had withdrawn from the right flank of the American first line had also taken up temporary positions to the right of Lawson's men. Like the British these formations were broken up by the woods, although they held positions in what approximated a single north–south line, bisecting the road at right angles. They had let the fleeing North Carolinians pass by them, and were ready and waiting for the British. Given the terrain, it was inevitable that the fighting on the second line would degenerate into a series of small actions in which groups of British regulars fought to come into contact with isolated groups of Virginian militia. Charles Stedman described this stage of the battle as "an action of almost infinite

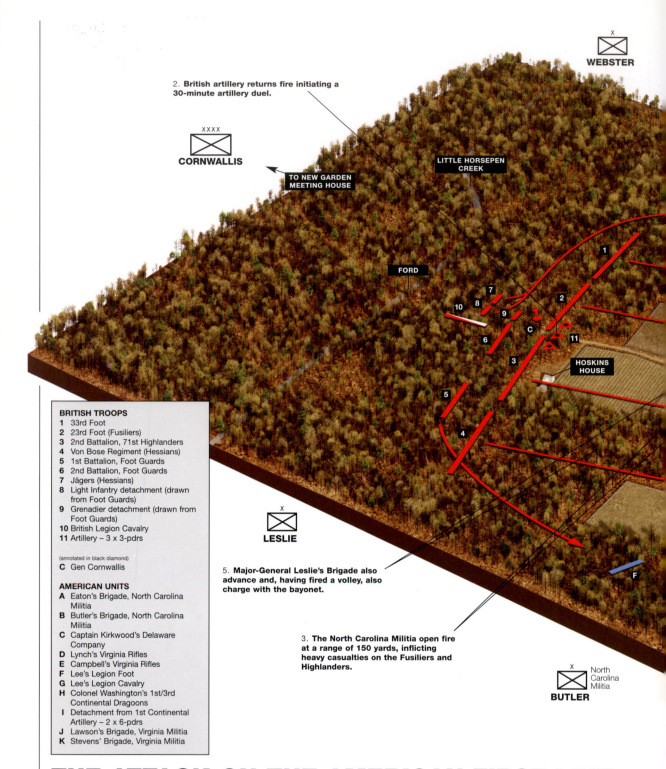

WEBSTER

2. British artillery returns fire initiating a 30-minute artillery duel.

CORNWALLIS

TO NEW GARDEN MEETING HOUSE

LITTLE HORSEPEN CREEK

FORD

HOSKINS HOUSE

LESLIE

5. Major-General Leslie's Brigade also advance and, having fired a volley, also charge with the bayonet.

3. The North Carolina Militia open fire at a range of 150 yards, inflicting heavy casualties on the Fusiliers and Highlanders.

North Carolina Militia

BUTLER

BRITISH TROOPS
1 33rd Foot
2 23rd Foot (Fusiliers)
3 2nd Battalion, 71st Highlanders
4 Von Bose Regiment (Hessians)
5 1st Battalion, Foot Guards
6 2nd Battalion, Foot Guards
7 Jägers (Hessians)
8 Light Infantry detachment (drawn from Foot Guards)
9 Grenadier detachment (drawn from Foot Guards)
10 British Legion Cavalry
11 Artillery – 3 x 3-pdrs

(annotated in black diamond)
C Gen Cornwallis

AMERICAN UNITS
A Eaton's Brigade, North Carolina Militia
B Butler's Brigade, North Carolina Militia
C Captain Kirkwood's Delaware Company
D Lynch's Virginia Rifles
E Campbell's Virginia Rifles
F Lee's Legion Foot
G Lee's Legion Cavalry
H Colonel Washington's 1st/3rd Continental Dragoons
I Detachment from 1st Continental Artillery – 2 x 6-pdrs
J Lawson's Brigade, Virginia Militia
K Stevens' Brigade, Virginia Militia

THE ATTACK ON THE AMERICAN FIRST LINE

15 March 1781, 1.00pm–2.00pm, viewed from the southeast showing the British attack on the first American defense line of North Carolina Militia. Although ordered to fire three volleys and then retire, the North Carolina Militia only manage one volley before being driven off, but they inflict heavy casualties on the advancing British.

6. Lieutenant-General Cornwallis orders the Jägers and the Light Infantry to support the British Left Wing.

4. The general advance of the British Foot comes to a halt as they fire a volley at the defending militia. Lieutenant-Colonel Webster then orders an attack with the bayonet.

1. American artillery opens the engagement by bombarding the British guns.

7. The American Right wing retires, reforming on the right flank of the American second line.

North Carolina Militia
EATON

RALLYING POINT

C

D

H

A

I

B

J

NEW GARDEN ROAD

K

TO HILLSBORO

GREENE

G

N

RALLYING POINT

9. While the American artillery retires the rest of the militia routs.

8. The American Left wing retires at the same time as the Right Wing.

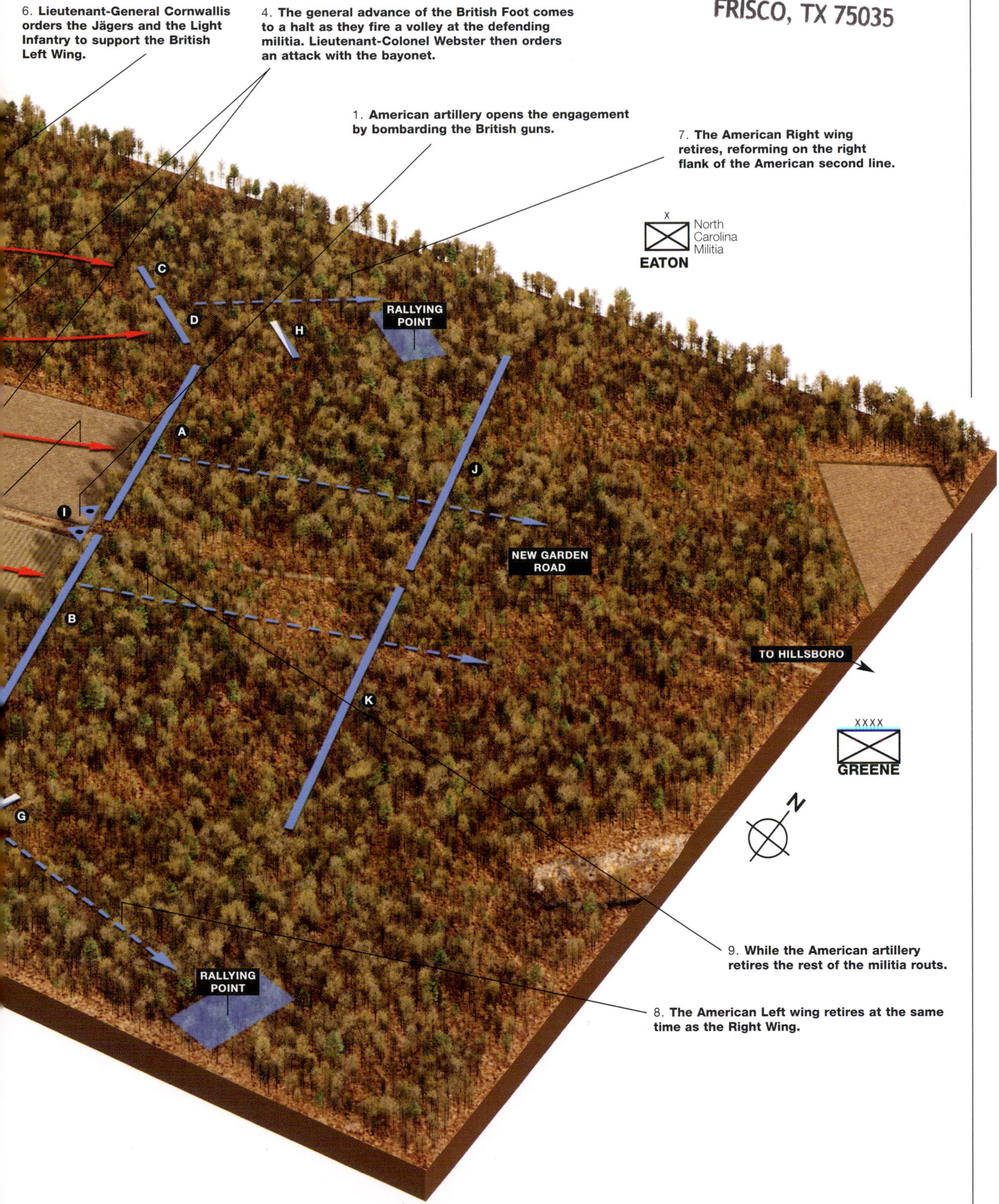

diversity." In other words, it was a confusing situation, a soldier's fight, where officers had little or no influence on the outcome of the fighting, save to encourage the men under their immediate command.

To the south of the road, General Leslie and his depleted 71st Highlanders faced odds of around four to one. The 150 or so Highlanders who remained came up against General Edward Stevens' 600 militiamen, who directed a "fierce and fatal" fire at the Scots. Many of the militiamen who opposed them were experienced regulars themselves, recently released from service in the Continental Army. The Highlanders had a tough fight on their hands. To the north, the 33rd Foot and 2nd Battalion, Foot Guards, made better progress against General Lawson's militia. Under the leadership of junior officers small groups of redcoats infiltrated the American line, Sergeant George Tucker of the Virginia militia discovering that the British had "gotten in our rear." He reported that this caused many of his fellow militiamen to run. In his words they "instantly broke off without firing a single gun and dispersed like a flock of sheep frightened by dogs." Pockets of resistance remained and fought back, but in general, the British pressed on through the woods, driving the Virginians before them. Between the two units, the 23rd Fusiliers were finding the going harder. Sir Thomas Saumarez, described that the militia in front of his men were "formed behind brushwood," creating a defensive position that was virtually unassailable. He ordered parties of fusiliers to work round to the left, circling the brushwood thicket and then attacking the Virginians from the flank and rear. Saumarez recalled: "they then attacked the enemy with the bayonet in so cool and deliberate a manner as to throw the Americans into the greatest confusion and disperse them." With this pocket cleared, the 23rd Fusiliers were able to make better progress and edged forward, although their advance still lagged behind the 33rd Foot and the Guards.

Sergeant Lamb of the 23rd was over on the right of his regiment's ragged line, probably some 250 yards north of the New Garden Road. He had also become separated from his unit, and although the woods to his right had already been cleared by the 2nd Battalion, Foot Guards, who were now somewhere up ahead through the trees, Lamb spotted small groups of American militia in the trees. He was filling his cartridge box from the ammunition of a dead guardsman when he spotted a lone mounted British officer. It was Major-General Cornwallis. Concerned at the slow progress made by the 71st Highlanders south of the road, he had ridden south to encourage his men. Instead, he was in imminent danger of riding into an ambush. His horse had already been shot under him, his present mount having been commandeered from a trooper in Tarleton's British Legion. As Lamb remembered: "His lordship was mounted on a dragoon's horse; the saddlebags were under the creature's belly, which much retarded his progress; owing to the vast quantity of underwood that was spread on the ground; his lordship was evidently unconscious of his danger." Sergeant Lamb raced forward, grabbed his commander-in-chief's bridle, and led his horse back to the north, and the safety of the main body of the 23rd Fusiliers.

To the north beyond the 33rd Foot, the German Jägers and the light companies of the Guards had come under heavy fire from Kirkwood's Delaware company and Lynch's Rifles. Sergeant Seymour of Kirkwood's

OVERLEAF

THE ATTACK ON THE AMERICAN FIRST LINE

The British attack on the first American militia line was delivered at 1.00pm with all the formal grace that was expected of a professional late-18th century army. On the left of the New Garden Road a hail of shot from Brig Eaton's North Carolina Militia stung the British regulars commanded by LtCol Webster and at one point it seemed as if the British attack would grind to a halt. Webster rode forward to encourage his men and the attack continued. The plate depicts the scene to the left of the American line, as the veteran infantry of the 71st Highlanders halt and prepare to fire a volley into the American ranks. On both sides of the road it was the American militia who fired first, causing heavy casualties amongst the advancing redcoats. As one American officer put it, the Highlanders "looked like scattered stalks in a wheatfield, when the harvest man had passed over it with his cradle." The three British and one Hessian regiment that formed the attacking line were undeterred, despite the brief hesitation of the units under Webster's command. On the British left the 71st Highlanders and the von Bose Hessian regiment to their right simply dressed their ranks,

filling the gaps in their line, then continued the advance. When the Highlanders got within 50 yards of the American positions, which ran along a split rail fence, they halted, presented their muskets and fired a single devastating volley. The British line is deployed in three ranks, the drums and colors having taken station to the rear, allowing the redcoats a clear field of fire. Similarly the regimental officers took a position immediately behind the rear rank. The scene depicts the right end of the Highland line, with to their right the left flank of the Hessian line approaching the second rail fence. Within a minute they will fire their own volley. The trail of dead and wounded left in their wake is testimony to the accuracy of the American fire. MajGen Leslie and his adjutant wear the uniforms of Highland officers, their mounts standing immediately behind the Highland right flank. The British volley broke the resistance of Brig Butler's American militiamen, who began to flee even before the Highlanders fired. Immediately after the volley the British line advanced towards the fence and, apart from a few stalwarts, the Americans fled the advancing bayonets. The British had broken the first line of enemy resistance, but at a heavy cost. (Adam Hook)

company remembered that, "our riflemen and musketry behaved with great bravery, killing and wounding great numbers of the enemy." Despite this fire they were being driven back by the equally galling fire of the British and German light troops. Washington's cavalry had already retired to its new position in support of Greene's third line, and some 30 minutes later, Kirkwood ordered his men to follow, after word came that the main Virginian line had collapsed. Despite the claims of Sergeant Seymour and others, the British light troops were outnumbered by a ratio of 3:2 in this northern sector of the battlefield. After about 30 minutes of hard fighting Colonel Webster's 33rd Foot and 2nd Guards Battalion (supported by the Guard Grenadier companies) managed to punch their way through Lawson's line, and the 23rd Fusiliers followed on behind, mopping up any last pockets of resistance. Soon afterwards the 71st Highlanders performed the amazing feat of driving back Stevens' militia south of the road, and the Virginians in this sector fled back towards the small ravine and the open fields beyond. General Edward Stevens of the Virginia militia had seen his militiamen run from the battlefield of Camden without firing a shot. As the General was taken to the rear, having being shot in the thigh, he had reason to be proud of the way his men had fought to redeem their honour. He later wrote: "The brigade behaved with the greatest bravery, and stood till I ordered their retreat." Of all the militia brigades on the field that day, Stevens' Virginians gave the best account of themselves against the Highlanders. It had been a hard-fought battle, and by this stage the Highlanders were in poor shape, and physically exhausted. Their officers stopped to rally them and dress their ranks some 400 yards beyond the line held by Stevens' militia. The battered Highlanders had lost half their strength.

Further to the south, the British soldiers of 1st Battalion, Foot Guards, were fighting their own private battle. Stedman recalled, "this

part of the British line was at times warmly engaged in front, flank and rear, with some of the enemy that had been routed in the first attack, and with part of the extremity of their left wing, which, by the closeness of the woods, had been passed unseen." In other words, the left flank of the Guards battalion had passed the southern extremity of Stevens' line. Although the British were unaware of the proximity of the Americans, some of the Virginia militia were able to track their opponents by the musketry of the men of Lee's Legion and Campbell's Rifles as they retreated. Samuel Houston, one of the Virginia militia, was part of a group who broke formation to attack the guardsmen as they passed. "We fired on their flank, and that brought down many of them … we pursued them about forty poles to the top of a hill, where they stood, and we retreated from them back to where we formed." This running fight ended when the Guards reached the small hillock where Lee and Campbell decided to make a stand. The guardsmen advanced up the slope, where the waiting Americans would appear on the summit, fire their muskets or rifles, then retire back to reload in safety. As British casualties mounted, it became clear that the Guards were in trouble. Once they reached the summit they drove off the riflemen at bayonet point, but then they came under fire from their flank, as Lee's infantry appeared through the woods. Most of the Guards officers had already been killed or wounded, and leaderless, the guardsmen retired to the crest of the hillock, then back down the far side, pursued by the re-formed American line. It looked like the small British unit would be overwhelmed when fresh troops appeared on their left flank, screening them from the men of Lee's Legion. Many of the Americans saw the blue coats of the newcomers and presumed they were regulars of the Continental Line, sent to help crush the British battalion. They realized their error when they called out the watchword "Liberty!" – the reply was a crushing volley of musketry. The blue-coated troops were the Hessian von Bose Regiment, and once again the tide of the private battle in the woods shifted in favour of the British. The battle raged on, but although the British now had the ascendancy, the fight was a tough one. As Stedman put it, after driving off an American unit, "they found it necessary to return and attack another body of them that appeared in their rear [and] in this manner they were obliged to traverse the same ground in various directions." Final British victory in this sector would only come when Cornwallis threw in his cavalry reserve to help drive Lee's men from the field.

The battle for the second American line was a hard-fought engagement in almost impossibly dense woods. Although the Virginian militia had been unable to stop the advance of Cornwallis's army, they had disordered their neat formations and had inflicted casualties. Witnesses recall that after the battle the woods on each side of the road were strewn with the dead and wounded of both armies, although the casualties had predominantly been British. Even worse for Cornwallis, a quarter of his remaining troops were isolated from the main battle, engaged in their own private struggle almost a mile to the south. So far the British had only faced militia, supported by regular light troops. The British troops knew that somewhere ahead of them lay the cream of the American army. Not only that, while the British were disorganized, battered and exhausted, the American regulars were fresh and eager for

ABOVE **This rather unflattering portrayal of Major-General Nathaniel Greene is based on a painting by Trumbul. The stocky commander of the American army at Guilford Courthouse demonstrated the ability of his defeated army to "rise and fight again."**

OPPOSITE **In this contemporary sketch map of the battle of Guilford Courthouse, the clearly defined troop dispositions were misleading. Greene was unable to influence the battle after his initial dispositions were made, while Cornwallis had no clear idea where the enemy lines were to be found, or even where elements of his own army were once the battle began.**

OVERLEAF

THE AMERICAN SECOND LINE – A BITTER FIGHT IN THE WOODS **As the British pursued the fleeing North Carolina militia into the woods their neat formations were broken up, as small groups of British soldiers followed clear paths through the trees, thickets and fallen logs. Consequently, when they reached the American second line, they arrived in small "penny packets," unable to rely on the massed firepower that had decided the issue minutes before at the split-rail fence. The Virginia militiamen of brigadiers Stevens (on the American left) and Lawson (to his right) contained a cadre of**

experienced Continental Army men whose time had expired, making them a tougher force than their Carolinian counterparts. As one British officer wrote of the fight in the woods it was, "an action of almost infinite diversity," a polite euphemism for uncoordinated and scrappy. The Virginians let the retreating North Carolina militiamen pass through their lines, then prepared themselves for the British regulars following on their heels. Firing was ragged, but the professionalism of the British proved decisive, as the advancing redcoats displayed a tactical flexibility that belied their stereotypical reputation as robotic disciples of linear tactics. The American line was not continuous, particularly on their right where small knots of Virginia Militia took positions behind fallen logs and thickets. The British response was to pin these islands of resistance with frontal fire, work their way around them, then attack the enemy at bayonet point from the flank and rear. This scene shows one such attack against a knot of Virginia militiamen of Brig Lawson's command, somewhere to the northwest of the New Garden Road, on the extreme right flank of the American line. Both sides took advantage of the cover provided by the woods and while line company troops of the British 33rd Foot led by a junior officer engage the enemy in a close-range musketry duel, the signs of battle to the British right indicate that other troops are trying to find a way around the American position. Although the Americans broke when faced with these unexpected British tactics, their fire took its toll of the redcoats and after the battle the woods were "carpeted" with the dead and wounded of both sides. After driving off the Virginia Militia, the British still had to face the third American line, and they would find the regulars of the American Continental Army a tougher nut to crack than the militiamen who manned the first two American lines. (Adam Hook)

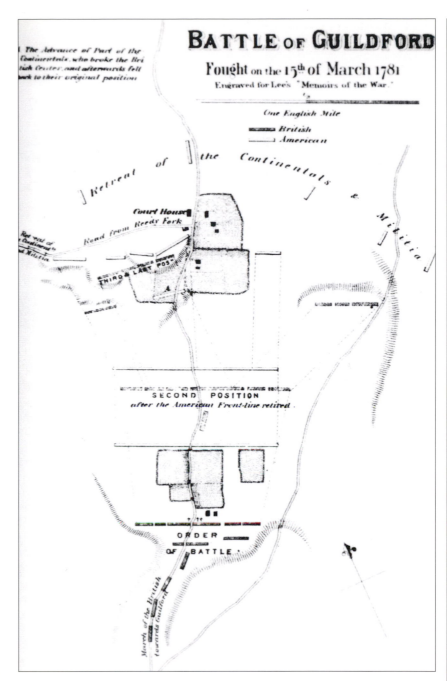

battle. The approaching climax of the battle would force the British to draw upon every last reserve of energy and professionalism to defeat their opponents. Meanwhile, Nathaniel Greene and his 1,400 regulars waited, watching the trees on the far side of the clearing in front of them.

THE THIRD LINE

As the Continental regulars of Greene's third defense line stood their ground facing west across the clearing in front of them, they must have

In this spirited depiction of American Continental Line infantry advancing, Howard Pyle captured the look and feel of a battlefield formation of the period, even though the illustration was drawn over a century after the war ended.

heard the sounds of battle creep closer to them through the trees. Shortly before 2.30pm, the first militiamen appeared on the far treeline, racing towards the regulars across the intervening 200 yards of open ground. It was clear that the British had defeated both lines of militiamen in front of them. Next, Kirkwood's Delaware company and Lynch's Rifles appeared through the woods to the north of the clearing, taking up position to the right of Colonel Greene's 4th Virginia Regiment on the extreme right of the American line. Washington's Continental dragoons followed behind them, crossing the open ground in front of the American lines before halting and turning about at the top of the ridge, some 250 yards south of the New Garden Road. Then came the British.

First to emerge were the Jägers and light infantry on the extreme north edge of the clearing, closely followed by the British 33rd Foot, directly in front of Brigadier-General Huger's Virginia brigade. These were Lieutenant-Colonel Webster's troops, less the fusiliers and the guardsmen who were still working their way through the woods just to the north of the road. Without waiting for either orders or reinforcements, Webster ordered his men forwards, pausing only to straighten their ranks. In an attack that "Light Horse Harry" Lee later described as one launched with "more ardour than prudence," Webster's three units advanced rapidly down the slope from the woods into the field, then headed straight for the waiting Virginians arrayed on the slope in front of them. Webster's men were hopelessly outnumbered, but it is probable he was unable to see any American troops apart from the ones directly in front of him, as small thickets of trees and scrub on the western slope of the clearing may have obscured Williams' Maryland brigade. The Continentals waited until the British were within point-blank range – probably somewhere around 20–40 yards – then fired a crushing volley. In the attack the British had veered slightly to the left, so while the light troops faced the 5th Virginia Regiment, Webster and the 33rd Foot were met by a volley from the 1st Maryland Regiment commanded by Colonel John Gunby. The volley

A black trumpeter in Colonel Washington's cavalry saves his commanding officer by firing his pistol at British horsemen. Detail from an 1845 oil painting of Cowpens. Washington's Continental dragoons wore white coats, not green ones. (State Capitol, South Carolina)

halted the British, and dead and wounded redcoats littered the field. One of the fallen was Webster himself, whose knee had been shattered by a musket ball. He had little option but to order a retreat and, as his men carried their Colonel to safety, the British left wing retired to the relative safety of the treeline.

Just as Webster ordered his men to retreat, more British troops emerged from the woods to the right of the 33rd Foot. The 2nd Battalion, Foot Guards, and the two attached companies of Guard Grenadiers had been commanded by Colonel O'Hara during the earlier phases of the battle. The colonel had been wounded twice, however, and had been sent to the rear. Command of the guardsmen had passed to Lieutenant-Colonel Charles Stuart of the 2nd Battalion, an experienced and capable officer. According to one account, Stuart and his men were "glowing with impatience to signalise themselves." As they emerged from the woods, the same thickets that had restricted Webster's view also served to screen the troops on the right of the American line. Probably all Stuart could see were the 2nd Maryland Regiment commanded by Colonel Benjamin Ford, and Captain Singleton's two 6-pdrs, which had been manhandled down the road to safety following the collapse of the first line. The guns stood in the middle of the road, some 300 yards away across the clearing. Stuart ordered his men to advance, with bayonets fixed. Colonel Otho Williams commanding the Maryland brigade watched as the men of the 2nd Maryland fired a single hasty volley at the advancing guardsmen,

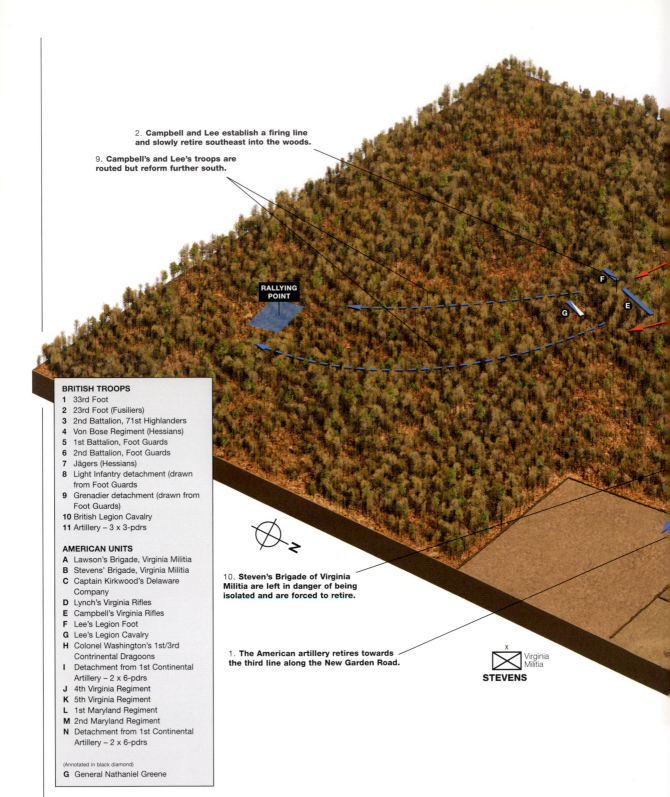

2. Campbell and Lee establish a firing line and slowly retire southeast into the woods.

9. Campbell's and Lee's troops are routed but reform further south.

RALLYING POINT

BRITISH TROOPS
1 33rd Foot
2 23rd Foot (Fusiliers)
3 2nd Battalion, 71st Highlanders
4 Von Bose Regiment (Hessians)
5 1st Battalion, Foot Guards
6 2nd Battalion, Foot Guards
7 Jägers (Hessians)
8 Light Infantry detachment (drawn from Foot Guards)
9 Grenadier detachment (drawn from Foot Guards)
10 British Legion Cavalry
11 Artillery – 3 x 3-pdrs

AMERICAN UNITS
A Lawson's Brigade, Virginia Militia
B Stevens' Brigade, Virginia Militia
C Captain Kirkwood's Delaware Company
D Lynch's Virginia Rifles
E Campbell's Virginia Rifles
F Lee's Legion Foot
G Lee's Legion Cavalry
H Colonel Washington's 1st/3rd Contrinental Dragoons
I Detachment from 1st Continental Artillery – 2 x 6-pdrs
J 4th Virginia Regiment
K 5th Virginia Regiment
L 1st Maryland Regiment
M 2nd Maryland Regiment
N Detachment from 1st Continental Artillery – 2 x 6-pdrs

(Annotated in black diamond)
G General Nathaniel Greene

10. Steven's Brigade of Virginia Militia are left in danger of being isolated and are forced to retire.

1. The American artillery retires towards the third line along the New Garden Road.

x
Virginia Militia
STEVENS

THE VIRGINIA MILITIA AND THE SECOND LINE

15 March 1781, 2.00pm–3.00pm, viewed from the northeast showing the confused fighting in the woods as the increasingly fragmented units of British regulars assault the American second line held by two brigades of Virginia Militia.

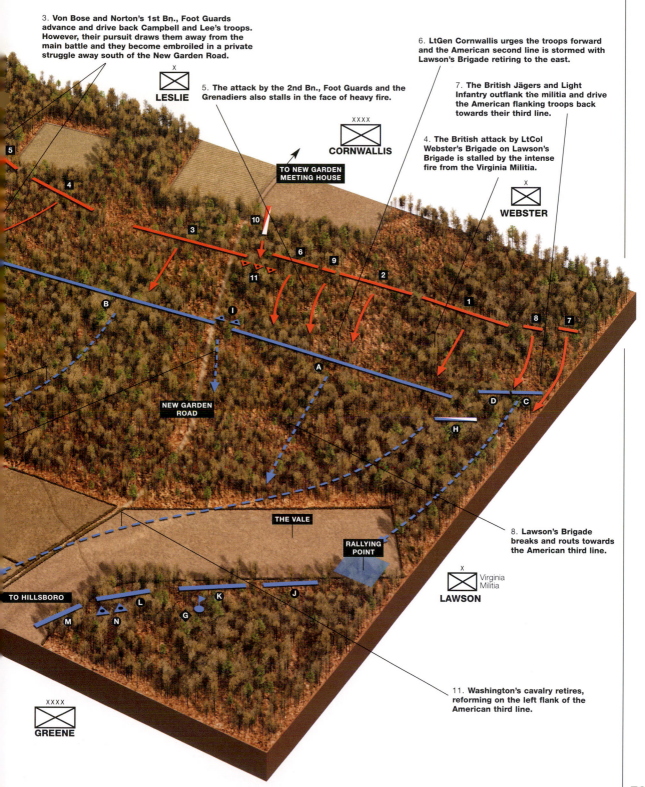

3. Von Bose and Norton's 1st Bn., Foot Guards advance and drive back Campbell and Lee's troops. However, their pursuit draws them away from the main battle and they become embroiled in a private struggle away south of the New Garden Road.

5. The attack by the 2nd Bn., Foot Guards and the Grenadiers also stalls in the face of heavy fire.

6. LtGen Cornwallis urges the troops forward and the American second line is stormed with Lawson's Brigade retiring to the east.

7. The British Jägers and Light Infantry outflank the militia and drive the American flanking troops back towards their third line.

4. The British attack by LtCol Webster's Brigade on Lawson's Brigade is stalled by the intense fire from the Virginia Militia.

x
LESLIE

xxxx
CORNWALLIS

TO NEW GARDEN MEETING HOUSE

x
WEBSTER

5

4

3

10

6

9

2

1

11

B

I

A

8

7

D

C

H

NEW GARDEN ROAD

THE VALE

RALLYING POINT

8. Lawson's Brigade breaks and routs towards the American third line.

x
Virginia Militia
LAWSON

TO HILLSBORO

M

N

L

G

K

J

11. Washington's cavalry retires, reforming on the left flank of the American third line.

xxxx
GREENE

79

In this fine depiction of a battlefield of the American War of Independence, General Greene is shown urging his troops to attack the British line. Although the battlefield depicted has been linked to Guilford Courthouse, the topography suggests it is more likely that it represents Eutaw Springs (1781).

then turned and ran. Stuart's men overran the two cannon and chased the Marylanders into the forest behind them. This was a pivotal moment in the battle. The Scottish Colonel had routed the left wing of Greene's third line, and the Guards were in a position to roll up the flank of the American position. If Webster's men launched another attack to pin the Continental Line, Greene would be powerless to prevent his army being destroyed in detail. Greene realized that his army was more important than any potential victory, and took the only course that would safeguard his most precious resource. He ordered a general retreat, sending a message to Colonel Greene's 4th Virginia Regiment to pull back from the line and to stand by to cover the army's retreat. What Greene failed to realize was the course of events was moving too swiftly for him to be able to influence the outcome of the battle. Cut off from communications, some of his subordinate commanders were unable or unwilling to obey his orders. One such unit was Colonel Gunby's 1st Maryland Regiment, who, hidden by thickets, had been passed by the Guards on the road. They now wheeled to face Stuart's men then advanced to catch the British in the flank. Gunby's deputy was Lieutenant-Colonel John Eager Howard, who wrote that Gunby "did not hesitate to order the regiment to face about, and we were immediately engaged with the guards. Our men gave them some well directed fires, and we then advanced and continued firing." The two battalions blazed away at each other at point-blank range. One observer recorded that; "This conflict between the brigade of guards and the first regiment of Marylanders was most terrific, for they fired at the same instant, and they appeared so near that the blaze from the muzzles of their guns seemed to meet." In the firefight Gunby's horse was shot, pinning the colonel and injuring him. Howard took command of the regiment, and elected to close the British and fight them hand-to-hand.

Howard later recalled that as he led the attack "I observed Washington's horse, and as their movements were quicker than ours, they first charged and broke the enemy." Colonel William Washington commanding the 1st and 3rd Continental Light Dragoons had been watching the charge of the British Guards and the rout of the 2nd Maryland Regiment. He decided the moment had come to intervene, and ordered his men to charge into the Guards' right flank. The cavalry had taken up position at the top of the slope to the south of the clearing, some 300 yards from Colonel Stuart's men. A young Virginian dragoon officer, Lieutenant Philemon Holocomb provided a description of the charge: "Leaping a ravine, the swords of the horsemen were upon the enemy, who were rejoicing in victory and safety, and before they suspected danger, multitudes lay dead."

Washington's men passed through the British ranks, which by this time were no longer in a rigid linear formation, but more closely resembled a wedge, with its apex at the edge of the forest, facing east. The Continental dragoons then wheeled around and returned, cutting their way back through the mass of British troops using their sabres. The hero of the moment was Peter Francisco, a young Virginia trooper who at over 6ft tall was regarded by his contemporaries as a giant. Using an extra-long sabre, he was credited with the felling of 11 guardsmen before he was unhorsed and wounded by a lunging bayonet. The 2nd Battalion, Foot Guards, were one of the most prestigious regiments in the British army, but their stoicism was severely tested by the double impact of Washington's cavalry, then the charging troops of the 1st Maryland Regiment. Colonel Howard wrote that: "my men followed very quickly, and we pressed through the Guards, many of whom had been knocked down by the horse without being much hurt. We took some prisoners, and the whole were within our power." Despite all this, the Guards fought on, surrounded by their enemies.

In a brutal melee, the Maryland regulars drove the Guards back from the treeline, around and past the two abandoned American 6-pdrs. The fighting ebbed into the clearing, with the Guards giving ground very slowly. In this swirling, brutal hand-to-hand scrum between the elite troops of both armies, one clash between a British and an American officer stands out in most accounts of the battle. Colonel Stuart was the de facto commander of both the 2nd Battalion, Foot Guards, and the attached two companies of Guard Grenadiers. Captain John Smith of the 1st Maryland was in the forefront of his regiment's drive into the flank of the Guards when Stuart confronted him. A description of the ensuing duel was provided by Colonel William R. Davie, the American Commissary-General: "Smith and his men were in a throng, killing the Guards and Grenadiers like so many furies. Colonel Stewart [sic], seeing the mischief Smith was doing, made up to him through the crowd, dust and smoke, and made a violent lunge at him with his smallsword … It

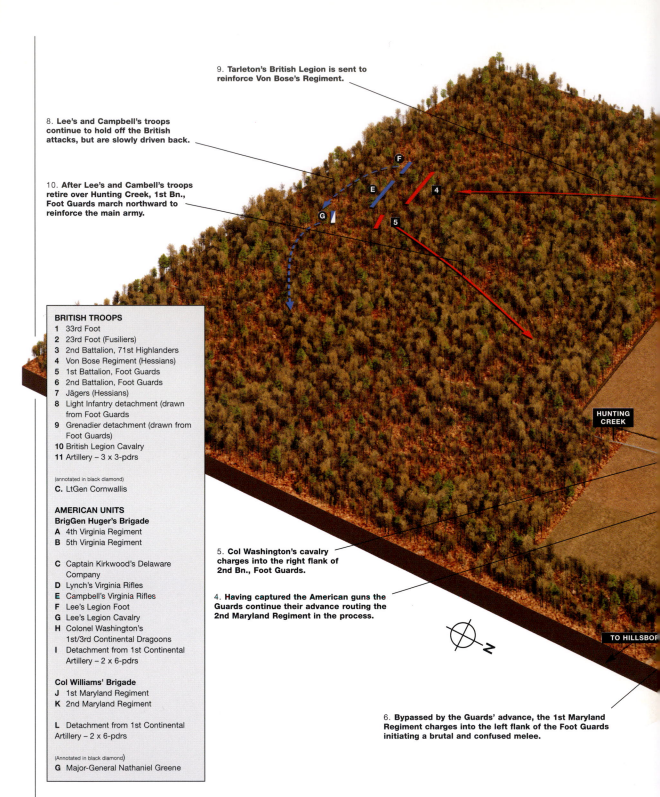

9. Tarleton's British Legion is sent to reinforce Von Bose's Regiment.

8. Lee's and Campbell's troops continue to hold off the British attacks, but are slowly driven back.

10. After Lee's and Cambell's troops retire over Hunting Creek, 1st Bn., Foot Guards march northward to reinforce the main army.

HUNTING CREEK

BRITISH TROOPS
1 33rd Foot
2 23rd Foot (Fusiliers)
3 2nd Battalion, 71st Highlanders
4 Von Bose Regiment (Hessians)
5 1st Battalion, Foot Guards
6 2nd Battalion, Foot Guards
7 Jägers (Hessians)
8 Light Infantry detachment (drawn
   from Foot Guards
9 Grenadier detachment (drawn from
   Foot Guards)
10 British Legion Cavalry
11 Artillery – 3 x 3-pdrs

(annotated in black diamond)
C. LtGen Cornwallis

AMERICAN UNITS
BrigGen Huger's Brigade
A 4th Virginia Regiment
B 5th Virginia Regiment

C Captain Kirkwood's Delaware
   Company
D Lynch's Virginia Rifles
E Campbell's Virginia Rifles
F Lee's Legion Foot
G Lee's Legion Cavalry
H Colonel Washington's
   1st/3rd Continental Dragoons
I Detachment from 1st Continental
   Artillery – 2 x 6-pdrs

Col Williams' Brigade
J 1st Maryland Regiment
K 2nd Maryland Regiment

L Detachment from 1st Continental
   Artillery – 2 x 6-pdrs

(Annotated in black diamond)
G Major-General Nathaniel Greene

5. Col Washington's cavalry charges into the right flank of 2nd Bn., Foot Guards.

4. Having captured the American guns the Guards continue their advance routing the 2nd Maryland Regiment in the process.

TO HILLSBOR

6. Bypassed by the Guards' advance, the 1st Maryland Regiment charges into the left flank of the Foot Guards initiating a brutal and confused melee.

REDCOATS VERSUS THE CONTINENTAL LINE

15 March 1781, 3.00pm–4.00pm, viewed from the northeast showing the brutal fighting as Cornwallis's battered troops confront General Greene's third line of American regulars, including the desperate action fough by the 2nd Battalion, Foot Guards against the 2nd Maryland Regiment and Colonel Washington's cavalry.

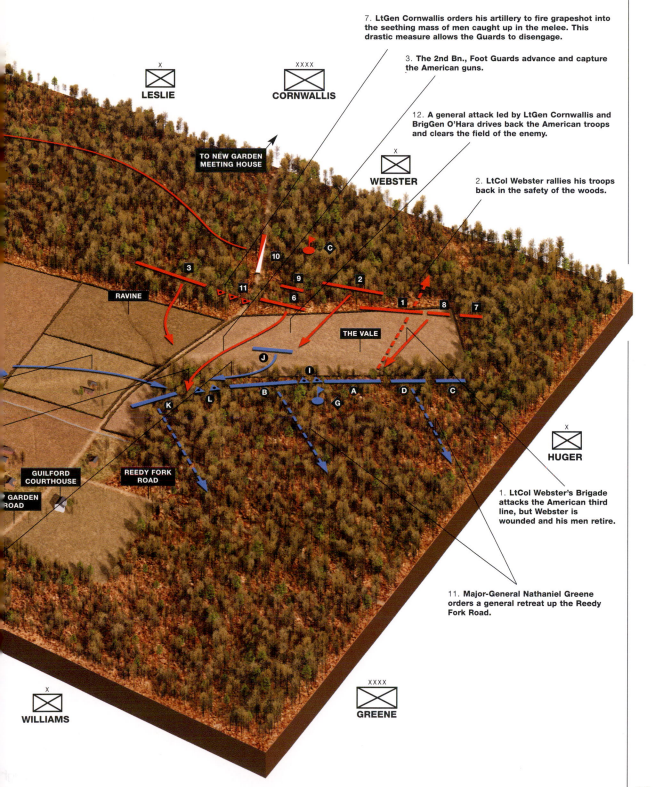

7. **LtGen Cornwallis orders his artillery to fire grapeshot into the seething mass of men caught up in the melee. This drastic measure allows the Guards to disengage.**

3. **The 2nd Bn., Foot Guards advance and capture the American guns.**

12. **A general attack led by LtGen Cornwallis and BrigGen O'Hara drives back the American troops and clears the field of the enemy.**

2. **LtCol Webster rallies his troops back in the safety of the woods.**

1. **LtCol Webster's Brigade attacks the American third line, but Webster is wounded and his men retire.**

11. **Major-General Nathaniel Greene orders a general retreat up the Reedy Fork Road.**

LESLIE

CORNWALLIS

WEBSTER

HUGER

WILLIAMS

GREENE

TO NEW GARDEN MEETING HOUSE

RAVINE

THE VALE

GUILFORD COURTHOUSE

REEDY FORK ROAD

GARDEN ROAD

would have run through his body but for the haste of the Colonel, and happening to set his foot on the arm of a man Smith had just cut down, his unsteady step, his violent lunge, and missing his aim brought him down to one knee on the dead man. The Guards came rushing up very strong. Smith had no alternative but to wheel around and give Stewart a back-handed blow over, or across the head, on which he fell." Stuart's staff sergeant attacked Smith, but was cut down by his American counterpart before another guardsman shot Smith in the back of the head. Carried from the field, Smith survived his horrific wound.

At one stage in the fight, Colonel Washington spotted a British officer riding out from the clearing near the road, followed by several mounted aides. He guessed it was Cornwallis himself, and he immediately led a party of dragoons off down the road to try to capture the British commander. Sensing the danger, Cornwallis turned about and retired to the safety of the 23rd Fusiliers, who were now emerging from the woods behind him. Washington gave up the chase and returned to the fray. Cornwallis had only needed a few moments to realize the peril his army was in. The Guards were being pushed back and were in danger of being overrun, while the left wing of his army was stalled on the treeline, their brigade commander incapacitated by a mortal wound. The Earl resorted to drastic measures. He called up Lieutenant MacLeod of the Royal Artillery, whose 3-pdrs had followed the army along the road as the battle flowed eastwards. Cornwallis ordered him to deploy his two available guns on the roadway as it entered the clearing, then to fire grapeshot into the melee raging some hundred yards in front of them. The British guns would be firing directly into the intermingled British and American troops. O'Hara tried to protest at this callous action, attempting to save his guardsmen. Cornwallis brushed aside the protest, and gave MacLeod the order to fire. The grapeshot scythed through the mass of men in front of the guns, cutting down soldiers of both sides by the score. What seemed an incredibly callous act was in fact the only resort left to Cornwallis if he was to avert a disaster. The canister shots forced the Marylanders and Washington's cavalry to recoil, leaving the battered guardsmen to retire to the safety of the treeline, passing the guns as they did so. At this point, two other British formations entered the battle. On the far right, the 71st Highlanders emerged from the woods to the south of the road, and marched straight across the fields towards the two American guns, and the re-forming gaggle of American cavalry. To the left of MacLeod's guns, the 23rd Fusiliers emerged from the woods and launched a fresh attack against the American line, which in turn encouraged the 33rd Foot and the light infantry to join them, creating a British line that stretched across the front of Huger's Virginia brigade. The wounded Webster led the fresh attack, ignoring his wounds. Meanwhile, O'Hara was busy rallying his guardsmen. Incredibly, they were reportedly keen to renew the attack. The tide of battle had turned, thanks to Major-General Cornwallis and Lieutenant MacLeod.

On the American side of the field, the 4th Virginia Regiment had already been pulled back towards the Reedy Fork Road. With the 2nd Maryland gone, that left the 5th Virginia and the bloodied 1st Maryland regiments to face the renewed British attack. Washington's cavalry were blown, and they would need time to reorganize themselves

OVERLEAF

THE AMERICAN THIRD LINE – THE CLIMAX OF THE BATTLE
When the first British units emerged from the woods in front of the American third line they were confronted with the serried ranks of American regular troops supported by both guns and horse. Undaunted they advanced to the attack only to be driven off by American musketry. The elite 1st Maryland Regiment commanded by Colonel John Gunby had pursued the British as they fell back, pushing ahead of the main American line in the center of the clear ground to the northwest of the New Garden Road. At this point the 2nd Battalion of the British Foot Guards arrived on the edge of the clearing, followed by Lord Cornwallis and the Royal Artillery battery. A stand of trees screened Col Gunby's men from LtCol Stuart's guardsman, so the Scottish officer ordered his men to advance straight down the road across the clearing towards the 2nd Maryland Regiment to their front. The Marylanders were supported by a battery of two 6-pdr guns. The Continental regiment fired one volley then turned and fled, leaving the guns to be captured by the advancing British. Stuart's guardsmen had now pressed well ahead of the rest of the British army, and faced a ragged American line to their left and two veteran American formations on either flank. The 1st Maryland Regiment charged the left flank of the 2nd Guards, initiating a brutal hand-to-hand melee. Colonel Washington's Continental Cavalry were deployed to the east, at the edge of the clearing and Washington ordered

his men to charge into the British right flank. The American dragoons passed clean through the British line, reaching the Marylanders behind them. They then returned, hacking their way through the now disorganized British. The scene depicts the guardsmen's frantic struggle for survival at that climax of the battle. To the left the experienced Continental regulars of the 1st Maryland Regiment are shown driving into the British ranks, after firing a series of highly-effective point blank volleys. Although the British fire was equally effective, the Americans had the advantage of cohesion and numbers, and the guardsmen were pushed back. Colonel Washington's Continental dragoons are shown hacking their way through the British formation, which could not turn to face the cavalry attack due to the assault of the Marylanders. The result was a brutal clash between horse and foot, fought with bayonets, pistols and cavalry sabers. Colonel Stuart fought a private duel with Captain Smith of the 1st Maryland Regiment and was cut down, only to be avenged by a guardsman who shot Smith in the head. Faced with the imminent defeat of one of his elite regiments Cornwallis ordered Lieutenant MacLeod of the Royal Artillery to fire grapeshot into the throng of troops – a brutal tactic that indiscriminately killed friend and foe but so stunned the Americans that the surviving guardsmen were able to retreat to safety. Fresh British reinforcements then turned the tide, and the now-disorganized American formations were forced to retreat, along with the rest of General Greene's army. (Adam Hook)

if they were to prove effective. Greene had little option but to reaffirm his earlier order for his army to conduct a general retreat. Both American regiments held the line as the rest of the army retired in reasonably good order to the north, harried by the relatively fresh 71st Highlanders and 23rd Fusiliers. The British finally recaptured Singleton's two 6-pdrs, along with two more guns, which the Americans had been forced to abandon further up the ridge to the north. Cornwallis had almost won the day, but the sounds of fighting still raged to the south, where the private war between the Hessians, Guardsmen and Lee's Legion was reaching a climax. As the rest of his army occupied the American positions around Guilford Courthouse, Cornwallis despatched Lieutenant-Colonel Tarleton and his British Legion to lend a hand in the fighting to the south.

While the attack on the American third line had been raging, "Light Horse Harry" Lee had been trying to prevent the 1st Battalion, Foot Guards, from disengaging and marching north to reinforce Cornwallis. Campbell's riflemen had been hard-pressed by the Hessians, who were firing volleys into the riflemen's ranks. The Virginians began to melt away, but several pockets remained, supported by a few militiamen. Lee tried to steal a march on Lieutenant-Colonel Norton of the Guards, and after pinning the von Bose Regiment, he tried to slip away to the east and north in an attempt to rejoin Greene's main army. He emerged from the woods ahead of the guardsmen, but looking across the fields he saw that Greene had already withdrawn, and the British were in possession of the field. Holding off the Hessians and Guards was now less important than ensuring his Legion survived to rejoin Greene. Consequently he continued to lead his men in a sweep around Guilford Courthouse, marching around the British to link up with Greene's rearguard. Back to the south, the Hessian commander ordered his men to "fire a volley upon the heaviest part of the militia," just when Tarleton's British Legion appeared behind the Hessian line. Tarleton charged, and as the Virginia militiaman Samuel Houston later recalled, "we were obliged to run, and many were sore chased, and some cut down." The fighting fizzled out in the south about 3.30pm, some 2½ hours after the battle began. The suffering would continue long after the smoke of battle had cleared.

Both militia lines had performed adequately, although the Carolinians would be criticized for not holding their ground for longer. The Continental regulars emerged from the fight with mixed laurels, with some regiments having performed heroically, while others ran in their first engagement. Above all, the American army had survived. Greene's words, "we fight, we get beat, rise and fight again" summed up the outcome of the battle. For the Americans, survival meant the hope of future victory. As for the British, the redcoats had performed magnificently. Frequently outnumbered and fighting in appalling terrain, they had cut their way through three successive American lines, proving their ability as some of the finest soldiers in the world. The only problem for Cornwallis was the cost. As the reports came in, he discovered a quarter of his small army lay dead or wounded in the woods and fields around Guilford Courthouse. For the British, it was a victory they could ill afford to win.

AFTERMATH

The American army retreated up the Reedy Fork Road, heading north from Guilford Courthouse. Three miles north, Greene reached Reedy Fork Creek, and it became clear that the British were not following in hot pursuit. He waited for several hours to collect stragglers and then continued on through the evening rain towards his old camp at the Speedwell Ironworks. The army reached the Ironworks on Troublesome Creek at dawn the morning after the battle. Eighteen miles to the south the British had spent a miserable, hungry night on the rain-sodden battlefield, surrounded by the dead and dying. The army spent the day burying the dead and collecting the wounded, who were evacuated to the New Garden Friends Meeting House. The American wounded were gathered at Guilford Courthouse, and word was sent to Greene to supply surgeons. The battlefield haul was impressive: 1,300 muskets, four cannon and piles of ammunition. Less satisfactory was the casualty list. The British lost 93 soldiers killed, 413 wounded and 26 missing. This total of 532 men represented over a quarter of Cornwallis's available troops. Of these, 64 of the wounded were serious and would take no further part in the campaign. Even worse, Cornwallis had lost gifted deputies in Lieutenant-Colonels Webster and Stuart, while Colonel O'Hara and Lieutenant-Colonel Tarleton were both wounded, leaving Cornwallis with a shortage of senior officers. By contrast, Greene lost 79 men killed, and 185 wounded. Most of the 1,046 missing Americans were militia, who might eventually return to the

"Cornwallis Retreating!" This 1781 pamphlet (broadside) was used to promulgate news of the battle to the American population. Leaflets of this kind were printed on the orders of both Washington and Congress in order to bolster morale. Despite its morale-raising function, the despatch quote in the broadsheet is surprisingly accurate.

Continental paper money of this kind was used to pay the soldiers and militiamen in Greene's army. Spanish gold coins were used as the coined currency on which these notes were supported, as the coins were internationally recognized as a monetary standard.

army. As Cornwallis counted his losses, he realized he was unable to continue his campaign for the Carolinas. There was not enough food and provisions, too many wounded, and too few men to conquer a continent. He had no option but to retreat to the safety of the coast. As Charles Fox, a British opposition politicians declared when he heard the news, "another such victory would ruin the British army."

Cornwallis planned to move his army to Bell's Mill on the Deep River, then to head south-east to Cross Creek, reaching the Cape Fear River. The army would then follow the river downstream to Wilmington, where the army could be provisioned. After leaving his severely wounded in the hands of local Quakers, Cornwallis marched his army out to Bell's Mill on 17 March. All this time, Greene's men were expecting to be attacked, and had entrenched along Troublesome Creek. When he discovered Cornwallis had begun marching, Greene wrote to the Governor of North Carolina, stating he was "not without hope of turning their victory into defeat." Despite his lack of militia he decided to give chase. On 19 March Greene ordered Lee's Legion to "hang upon the rear" of Cornwallis's army as it marched south. He followed on behind with the rest of his army. On the way the seriously wounded American soldiers were also left in the hands of the long-suffering Quakers. Cornwallis reached Bell's Mill on 19 March where his army rested for two days to gather food, then they pressed on towards Ramsay's Mill. Local loyalists were shocked at the bedraggled appearance of the army, and despite assurances that the British had won, they failed to flock to the colors. At Ramsey's Mill Cornwallis ordered a bridge to be constructed across the Deep River, and his troops crossed on 28 March, just hours ahead of Greene's army. The bridge was burned behind them as the British pushed on towards the Cape Fear River. When he reached the burnt bridge, Greene decided to give up the pursuit. There was no chance of him catching Cornwallis, and his troops would be put to better use elsewhere.

On reaching Cross Creek, Cornwallis and his battered little army followed the Cape Fear River, finally entering Wilmington on 7 April. The port had fallen into British hands three months before, captured by troops sent north from Charleston, and it proved a rallying point for local loyalists. Cornwallis had reached a safe haven, with food, supplies, communications and the promise of reinforcements. In Wilmington word reached his headquarters that General Greene had been marching his army southwards towards South Carolina. Cornwallis had the option of shipping his army south to counter Greene's move, but he felt the troops left behind to garrison the state were sufficient to hold off the Americans, with loyalist help. For his part, Cornwallis began to consider plans for the conquest of Virginia, the state he considered was the key to the American colonies. Virginia was the most populous and prosperous of all the American colonies, and Cornwallis argued that once in British hands, all resistance to the south would wither and die, while Washington's troops to the north would be starved of precious manpower, provisions and resources. The seeds had been sown for the campaign that would lead Cornwallis to Yorktown six months later. With 1,435 soldiers fit and ready for duty, Cornwallis planned to capture the lynchpin of a continent. On 25 August 1781 he led his men north on the long road to disaster and defeat.

In most American towns and cities nightwatchmen were used to spread news about the course of the war. Word of the battle of Guilford Courthouse reached Philadelphia some two weeks after the battle was fought.

By failing to defeat Nathaniel Greene's army, Cornwallis had committed a strategic error which cost Britain the very southern colonies his men fought so hard to keep. While the British marched to the coast and re-established their supply lines, General Greene used his nucleus of Continental Army regulars to forge a new army, gathered from the militia of the Carolinas as he marched south. Although defeated at the battle of Hobkirk's Hill near Camden on 25 April 1781, a defeat for which Colonel Gunby of the 1st Maryland Regiment became Greene's scapegoat, his army rallied and resumed its offensive. He continued to mop up Loyalist and British strongholds in South Carolina for another six months then, following another defeat at Eutaw Springs on 8 September, he displayed his ability to "rise and fight again" by forcing the British to withdraw to the immediate hinterland of Charleston. By the time Greene had finished his conquest of the Carolinas, Cornwallis was defeated, having been trapped at Yorktown by a joint Franco-American army.

Tactically Cornwallis won the battle of Guilford Courthouse, but at every stage during the campaign it was Greene, not his experienced British rival, who displayed a flair for strategy. Given his small army and the vast distances over which it was forced to march, Cornwallis and his British fought brilliantly, and almost achieved the impossible. Unfortunately for the British cause, and the thousands of Carolinians who remained loyal to the crown, this was not enough. While Cornwallis outfought Greene, the latter outmaneuvered and ultimately outwitted his aristocratic opponent. The battle of Guilford Courthouse might have been won when Cornwallis ordered his artillery to open fire at a crucial juncture of the battle. The war for the southern colonies was won when Greene emerged from the battle with his army virtually intact.

THE BATTLEFIELD TODAY

The New Garden Road, running through the centre of the battlefield, with pine woods on either side. Although the trees were less dense in 1781, the photograph gives a good impression of the terrain in which the battle was fought. The photograph was taken just in front of the location of Greene's second defensive line.

Most of the battlefield of Guilford Courthouse now forms part of the "Guilford Courthouse National Military Park," a site run by the US Department of the Interior's National Park Service. In 1886 Judge David Schenck of Greensboro, North Carolina, purchased 30 acres of land on the battlefield, in order to save the site for posterity. By the following year the Guilford Battle Ground Company had been formed to administer the site, and over the years more land was added, monuments were erected, and a small museum displaying relevant artefacts was opened to the public. Through the efforts of the company, the Federal Government passed legislation through Congress to have the site recognized as being of national significance, and in 1917 the Guilford Courthouse National Military Park was created. The Guilford Battle Ground Company duly deeded its lands to the government, and then disbanded. Between 1917 and 1933 the park was administered by the Secretary of War. At that point it was transferred to the Department of the Interior, to be run by the National Park Service. Since then, the National Park Service has attempted to expand their holdings, and to restore the battlefield to its historic setting. That involved planting trees to give the area the semblance of the open woodland that existed on the site in 1781, and recreating some of the salient features of the battlefield. These include the delineation of the line of the New Garden Road, and the clearing in front of the American third line of defence.

Today, the Guilford Courthouse National Military Park comprises approximately 149 acres of land, which includes much of the original battlefield, and extends to include the site of the original Guilford Courthouse, which no longer exists. The site of the building is indicated by interpretative panels for visitors. Scattered throughout the park are some 29 monuments and memorials, including the well-known equestrian statue of Major-General Nathaniel Greene. A new and substantial Visitors' Center provides a display and interpretation area, a movie theater that provides a background to the campaign and the battle, and a superb museum gift store. The National Park Service staff on duty are extremely knowledgeable, and will be able to answer just about any question about the battle you could ask, or at least point you in the direction of someone who can provide further information.

The battlefield is difficult to reach, but well worth the effort. Most visitors will arrive in the Greensboro area on Interstate 40 (which passes through Asheville and Raleigh, North Carolina), or the Interstate 85 (which connects Charlotte, North Carolina with Richmond, Virginia). Both connect on the south side of the city (Exit 219 on I-40, or 123 on I-85). Take I-85 east to Exit 127, then drive north on the State Road 29 for 3 miles until its junction with Route 70 (W. Wendover Avenue), then follow it west. If travelling into the area from the I-40 heading east, take

Exit 124 (Wendover Avenue), then follow it east. Both roads intersect with US 220, which heads north. Appropriately enough, this road is called Battleground Avenue. Three miles north of the junction with Wendover Avenue you'll find signs to the Guilford Courthouse National Military Park, which asks you to turn right on to New Garden Road and into the Visitors' Center car park. Alternatively, you can drive up Old Battleground Road, then turn left. Congratulations. You found it!

The Visitors' Center is located in open woods, approximately 100 yards to the east of the first American defense line, and is the starting point for the walking or driving tour of the battlefield. Turning out of the Center the drive curves west to the Forbis Monument, sited at the centre of the position held by Butler's North Carolina militia during the first phase of the battle. Incidentally, the first battlescene in this book (see p.70–71) is set on the same spot. Captain Arthur Forbis of Guilford County was mortally wounded on the spot, after the 71st Highlanders and the von Bose Regiment stormed his position by the rail fence. The road takes you in a loop over the ground held by Campbell's Rifles and Lee's Legion (passing the grave of Captain Tate of Campbell's unit), it then returns you to the Old Battleground Road. After crossing over the public road, you enter the eastern portion of the park. This is the wooded ground that lay between the first and second American lines. After 125 yards, visitors will reach a point that bisects the American second line. A foot trail from the parking place there leads off through the woods towards the monument to General Greene, which overlooks the site of the New Garden Road. At this point the visitor is standing approximately on the spot where Brigadier-General Stevens of the Virginia militia was wounded, and where the 71st Highlanders pushed back the Virginians. The second battlescene in this book (see p.74–75) is set roughly in the same area. The running fight and stand by Lee's Legion and the British right wing took place in the ground now occupied by the Forest Lawn Cemetery, beyond the park to the south. Further on where the road bends was the spot where the woods gave way to the open fields to the south of the Guilford Courthouse clearing. At this spot is a monument to Major Joseph Winston of Surrey County, who

The Continental Line of Greene's third defense line stood on this small ridge. Although the woods have encroached upon the battlefield, enough of the "natural amphitheatre" of this part of the battlefield survives for visitors to trace the course of events.

This memorial to Colonel Stuart of the 2nd Battalion, Foot Guards, was erected on the site of his death, in front of the main American line, and just north of the New Garden Road.

BELOW The description of the clearing where the final stage of the battle was fought as a "natural amphitheatre" is appropriate, given the slope on both sides of the road and off to the left (west). The photograph is taken from the position occupied by Colonel Washington's cavalry when they charged the British Foot Guards in the hollow below them. The markers on the right of the clearing denote the positions occupied by the main American line.

is buried close to the road. The death of Richard Taliaferro of his command was probably the last fatality of the battle, and a marker honours both men. The town of Winston-Salem was subsequently named after the Major. Two-hundred-and-fifty yards down the drive to the northeast is a tall granite obelisk which marks the position occupied by Colonel Washington's Continental dragoons after they retired from their position on the first defensive line. From this spot Washington launched his charge into the right flank of the 2nd Battalion, Foot Guards. It also provides a superb view over the "natural amphitheatre" where the final stage of the battle took place. The open field is much smaller now than it was in 1781, but the salient features of this crucial arena can still be seen today. The ground slopes down from the monument until it reaches the line of the New Garden Road, then it rises again to the left and right. Visitors on foot can walk around the footpath to the left, which intersects the footpath that follows the course of the small ravine from General Greene's monument. Further on, where the road emerges from the woods, several monuments honour the contributions made by the men of Delaware and Maryland. Although the west side of the clearing is roughly in the same place as it was in 1781, the northern boundary comes to within 50 yards of the line of the road, bisecting the position held by the 5th Virginia regiment. The remainder of the American right wing extended off to the north. Right in the centre of the present open field is a monument to Colonel James Stuart of the Foot Guards, who was killed during hand-to-hand combat with the 1st Maryland Regiment on that spot. The visitor is now standing on the spot where the 2nd Battalion of the Foot Guards was assaulted by both the Marylanders and by Washington's cavalry. This scene is depicted in the third battlescene in this book. A few yards to the east is the position held by the main American line, with a replica field piece marking the position occupied by the American guns during the final stage of the battle. Returning to the drive, visitors are taken past the site of Guilford Courthouse itself. The courthouse was abandoned in 1808, as a new building in Winnsboro served as the new judicial centre for the county. Nothing now remains, save markers denoting the extent of the original structure, and the historic route of the Reedy Fork Road, used by the American army in their retreat. The drive curves back in a loop to the north and west, taking visitors to a monument marking the third line and the position occupied by Major-General Greene during the battle. From here the road curves slightly south towards the Greene Monument, crossing the ground held by the Lawson's Viriginia militia during the second stage of the battle. It then recrosses Old Battleground road, and returns you to the Visitors' Center. One more feature is worth a visit. Further to the west down New Garden Road from the Visitors' Center (and outside the Park) is the Hoskins House, the only structure from the battle that still remains standing today. This site, where the British right wing formed up before attacking the first American line, is privately owned. For visitors wanting to discover other sites relevant to the campaign, Daniel W. Barefoot's superb book *Touring North Carolina's Revolutionary War Sites* (Winston-Salem, NC, 1998) is available in the Visitors' Center, and the Park Rangers will be happy to help you in your quest. For more information, contact the park on (336) 288-1776, or visit its website at www.nps.gov/guco.

BIBLIOGRAPHY

The following titles are all either readily available, or can be found with a little persistence in specialist or second-hand (used) bookstores. All of the published contemporary sources listed here are available in both the British Library in London, or the Library of Congress in Washington, DC.

Secondary Sources

(including readily available and reprinted contemporary sources)

Thomas E. Baker, *Another such Victory: The story of the American defeat at Guilford Courthouse*, Eastern Acorn Press (New York, NY, 1981)

Daniel W. Barefoot, *Touring North Carolina's Revolutionary War Sites*, John F. Blair Publishing (Winston-Salem, NC, 1998)

Daniel W. Barefoot, *Touring South Carolina's Revolutionary War Sites*, John F. Blair Publishing (Winston-Salem, NC, 1999)

Mark M. Boatner III, *Encyclopaedia of the American Revolution*, Stackpole Books (Mechanicsville, PA, 1992). Originally published by David McKay Company, 1966

John Buchan, *The Road to Guilford Courthouse: The American Revolution in the Carolinas,* John Wiley & Sons (New York, NY, 1997)

Earl J. Coates and James L. Kochan, *Don Troiani's Soldiers of North America, 1754–1865*, Stackpole Books (Mechanicsburg, PA, 1998)

Anthony D. Darling, *Red Coat and Brown Bess*, Museum Restoration Service (Bloomfield, Ontario, 1971)

S. James Gooding, *An Introduction to British Artillery in North America,* Museum Restoration Service (Bloomfield, Ontario, 1972)

Henry Lee, *The American Revolution in the South*, Arno Press (New York, NY, 1969). Originally published as *Memoirs of the War in the Southern Department*, 1827

Dan L. Morrill, *Southern Campaigns of the American Revolution*, Nautical & Aviation Publishing (Mount Pleasant, SC, 1993)

George C. Neumann, *Battle Weapons of the American Revolution: The Historian's Complete Reference*, Scurlock Publishing (Texarcana, TX, 1998)

George C. Neumann & Frank J Kravik, *Collector's Illustrated Encyclopaedia of the American Revolution*, Scurlock Publishing (Texarcana, TX, 1997)

John S. Pancake, *This Destructive War: The British Campaign in the Carolinas, 1780–1782*, University of Alabama Press (Tuscaloosa, AL, 1992)

Hugh F. Rankin, *The North Carolina Continentals,* University of North Carolina Press (Chapel Hill, NC, 1971)

Warren Ripley, *Battleground: South Carolina in the Revolution*, Evening Post Publishing (Charleston, SC, 1983)

George F. Scheer & Hugh F. Rankin, *Rebels and Redcoats*, Cleveland Press (Cleveland, OH, 1957)

John Selby, *The Road to Yorktown*, Hamish Hamilton Press (London, 1976)

Banastre Tarleton, *A History of the Campaigns of 1780 and 1781 in the Southern Provinces of North America*, Ayer Publishers (North Stratford, NH, 1999). First published in London, 1787

W.J. Wood, *Battles of the Revolutionary War, 1775–1781*, Algonquin Books (Chapel Hill, NC, 1990)

Contemporary Sources

Charles Caldwell, *Memoirs of the Life and Campaigns of the Hon. Nathaniel Greene* (Philadelphia, PA, 1819)

Sir Henry Clinton; *Observations on Mr. Stedman's History of the American War* (London, 1794)

William Gordon, *The History of the Rise, Progress and Establishment of the Independence of the United States of America* Vol. III (New York, 1801)

Roderick Mackenzie, *Strictures on Lt. Col. Tarleton's History of the Campaign of 1780 and 1781 in the Southern Provinces of North America* (London, 1787)

Charles Stedman, *The History of the Origin, Progress and Termination of the American War* Vol II (Dublin, 1794)

INDEX